Garland F. Pinholster

Athletic Director
Oglethorpe University

ENCYCLOPEDIA

OF

BASKETBALL

DRILLS

Englewood Cliffs, N. J.

PRENTICE-HALL, INC.

Fifteenth printing ....*September, 1967*

Acknowledgements

I owe something to every administrator who has entrusted me with the task of teaching basketball. I owe something to every player who has ever played with me, for me, or against me. It is absolutely necessary to give particular thanks to the following: Coach Bob Polk of Vanderbilt University; Coach Glenn Wilkes of Stetson University; Coach Ed Diddle, Jr. of Middle Tennessee State College; Coach Jim Hinson of Atlanta; Coach Bill Yoast of Roswell, Georgia; and Dr. Ben Bonhorst of Oglethorpe University.

To do complete justice to the last person, I should probably list her as co-author. She has acted as proofreader, typist, illustrator, and inspirer. To my wife Caroline, thanks; and my grateful appreciation is herewith extended to every coach and player who has taken the time to stop and "talk basketball" with me.

GARLAND F. PINHOLSTER

Dedication

To my mother

I affectionately dedicate this book

The Book ... The Author ...
And You

You, the basketball coach, are vitally interested in the teaching of fundamental drills for effective development of the individual player and the team. This book will serve you as an invaluable assistant coach.

Whether you have been coaching basketball for a year or fifteen years, you will discover drills to fit your style of play. Coach Pinholster, one of the most energetic and promising young coaches in the country, has included drills that cover all phases of the game. Each chapter begins with the simple drills and progresses to the more complex drills. This sequence will greatly aid the coach in using the book as a guide to overcoming player and team weaknesses.

As an aid in helping to organize daily practice schedules, as a conserver of time, and as a source of a wide variety of basketball drills, this book fills a great need. In drawing from its contents, you will be aiming at a more balanced, efficient team and also at a higher figure in the all-important "wins" column.

BOB POLK
Head Basketball Coach
Vanderbilt University

CONTENTS

Part I

CONDITIONING, PRACTICE, AND WARM-UP DRILLS

3. BEFORE-GAME WARM-UP DRILLS (Cont.)

Part II
DRILLS FOR TEACHING
OFFENSIVE FUNDAMENTALS

4. SHOOTING DRILLS   31

5. PASSING DRILLS   51

12. TWO AND THREE MAN SCORING DRILLS (Cont.)

Part IV
TACTICAL SITUATION DRILLS

Part I

CONDITIONING, PRACTICE, AND WARM-UP DRILLS

1

Pre-Season
Conditioning Program

Every basketball coach strives unceasingly to get extra effort, concentration, and desire to win from his team. These "extras" are the marks of distinction displayed by champions; they are the marks of hard work.

Symbolic of such extra effort is the off-season training program. Teams that undergo a spring, fall, or summer training session will certainly come closer to that promised land of basketball—the championship.

Football teams have an additional season during the spring. The baseball season extends from February to October. Track men have an opportunity to run cross-country during the fall. So why not an additional training season for basketball? Often the regular season is so cramped with game competition that the time left for work on fundamentals is extremely limited. Some conference rules would restrict fall practice, but the spring or summer seasons would serve just as well.

Off-season practice provides a strong indication to your players that this is to be a year of intense and concentrated endeavor. They understand that you mean to come as close as possible to the attainment of the team's basketball potential. As a result, they will develop a positive attitude. They'll become more receptive to instruction. Early season mistakes will be cut to a minimum, and

3

physical disabilities such as weak ankles and sore feet will be eliminated. Team morale will be high because the players will have ample opportunity to "prove" themselves to the coach before the first game.

Best results from pre-season training are obtained where specific objectives are set up. It's then possible to map out a schedule that will bring about greater improvement than haphazard "scramble" sessions. Though every coach has his own ideas with regard to the practice session, there are some things all coaches would agree upon. Here are several of the more universal ideas concerning the purpose of off-season practice:

1. Improvement of jumping ability.

With proper exercise, each boy can increase his vertical height on a standing jump by three inches or more. Since rebounding is so important, this aim alone should be enough to convince the conscientious athlete that these additional practice hours are a good investment.

2. Development of circulo-respiratory endurance or stamina.

Whether you fast break or slow break, the value of having plenty of "wind" can never be underestimated. Many victories have been earned simply through superior condition.

3. Increase of muscular strength.

The day of the tall, slim, weak player is passing rapidly. A boy may be thin, but he needs great tensile strength in all his muscle tissue. Without such strength his defensive and rebounding effectiveness will be lessened.

4. Improvement of agility and coordination.

These qualities epitomize basketball. They *are* basketball. Without them, a boy will never become a great player. Fortunately, these abilities can often be developed. Certainly they can be improved.

5. Development or improvement of split vision.

A youngster can have all sorts of eye defects and still become a good athlete if he can see laterally. Some great performers seemingly have eyes in the backs of their heads. They may appear to pass blindly, without looking in the direction of their receivers. They have developed peripheral vision to a high degree of functional efficiency.

6. Acquisition of a thorough knowledge and understanding of the rules.

As a coach or player, you will have other reasons for working overtime. But these few objectives, pursued religiously, will reap great dividends.

Physical fitness tests should be given at the beginning and end of the program to determine its success. The Sargent Jump Test is a most reliable method of measuring jumping ability. Other tests that may prove useful are the timed squat thrust for coordination, squat jump for agility, and timed distance run for testing circulo-respiratory endurance.

A written test offers the best way to measure knowledge of the rules, and most driver training schools have a device for checking peripheral vision.

Here is a six-weeks fall conditioning program for basketball. It can be amended to cover situations where time, over-all athletic program, and player weakness might warrant.

First Week

Monday: Give each athlete a rule book and make an assignment. Administer and record all tests.

Tuesday, Wednesday and *Thursday:*
  1. Calisthenics (6 repetitions).
  2. Thirty-minute volleyball game.
  3. Basketball fundamentals (15 minutes).
  4. Alternately run and walk for one mile.

Friday: The same workout as the three preceding days plus a written test covering the weekly rules assignment.

The volleyball game should be officiated carefully during this week. Teamwork and increased skill will make this an enjoyable period of recreation. On each succeeding week through the fifth week, a rules assignment will be given on Monday and tested on Friday.

Second Week

Daily Workout:
  1. Calisthenics (6 repetitions).
  2. Thirty-minute volleyball game.

3. Fundamentals (20 minutes).
4. Run one mile.

Notice that the difficulty and strenuousness of the workout is being gradually increased.

Third Week

Daily workout:

1. Calisthenics (7 repetitions).
2. Thirty-minute volleyball game.
3. Fundamentals (20 minutes).
4. Run one-half mile, then alternately run and walk a full mile.

Fourth Week

Daily workout:

1. Calisthenics (8 repetitions).
2. Fifteen-minute volleyball game.
3. Run split vision drills with medicine ball for about 6 minutes.
4. Fundamentals (30 minutes).
5. Run one mile, then alternately run and walk another mile.

Fifth Week

Daily workout:

1. Calisthenics (9 repetitions).
2. Fifteen-minute volleyball game.
3. Medicine ball split-vision drills.
4. Fundamentals (30 minutes).
5. Run two miles.
6. Give test covering entire rule book.

Sixth Week

Monday, Tuesday, Wednesday:

1. Calisthenics (10 repetitions).
2. Fifteen-minute volleyball game.
3. Medicine ball split-vision drills.

4. Fundamentals (30 minutes).
5. Run two and one-half miles.

Thursday: Complete rest.

Friday: Administer and record all tests.

Some recommended calisthenics for basketball players are: bend and reach, squat thrust, high jumper, squat jumper, lunger, finger-tip push-ups.

Strict adherence to good form should be maintained while performing the calisthenics. Unless your athletes perform these movements properly in the early stages of training, they will find them unusually difficult as the number of repetitions is increased. Executed correctly, they'll become easier as the weeks pass because of added strength. Though some boys will complain about the calisthenics, most of these same lads really have a deep-rooted desire to achieve good physical condition and will take great pride in their new physical development later in the season.

After a week of training the coach can conduct specialized weight-lifting exercises for boys who require something more than calisthenics. This can be accomplished while the others are playing volleyball.

Conducting the workout outdoors will add variety to your program. All types of competition help keep spirit high, as well as encouraging participation and eliminating boredom. If it is possible to obtain the help of a qualified dance teacher, modern dance can also be used profitably in the pre-season program to create interest and as a conditioner. This should be attempted only by a trained person who has received pointers on the major aims and objectives of such a program from the coach.

Given a week of absolute rest at the close of the conditioning program, the boys will then be eager and ready to start regular practice.

2

Planning Your Daily Practice

Why Practice?

The average athlete will ask himself many times during an athletic season, "Why all this hard work, sweat, and even physical pain?" He sees beginning players with much natural talent become seemingly efficient overnight. His increase in skill appears so small in comparison with another person's ability. Coaches are not always as patient and understanding as the girl friend. Star players' practice efforts aren't always overwhelming. The fellow he has to guard or outrun appears to be unusually talented. Climatic conditions seem to warrant no exercise more strenuous than checkers.

Ask Roger Bannister why practice is necessary. John Landy, Bob Richards, George Mikan, Stan Musial and Bob Cousy are all fellows who can give you some of the answers. These are men who have completed the cycle of train-perform, train-perform until they became champs. They know the thrill of throwing a press against a tough opponent for a win in the closing minutes of a game. They can tell you how it feels to run the best mile in the history of man. You will see why championships are not cheap. An understanding and appreciation of training is a primary requirement for the champ. The answers they will give won't all sound alike, but you will be able to recognize their mutual respect for practice.

The outstanding baseball player cannot be worrying about his batting stance if he expects to hit the ball. A pivot man won't score if he has to think about each step he takes. Pole vaulters would never clear 15 feet while reviewing hand position on the pole. The quarterback who has to follow the ball with his eyes on a hand-off is lost. So one answer to this question of the need for practice is that good athletic movements must be *automatic*. They must be reflex action. Action of this type should be performed over and over until the muscle responds as *mechanically* as the transmission in an automobile. Constant drill is needed. Attention to detail and repeated correction of errors are required.

A great football player will not perform well in that all-important last quarter if he is tired. Fatigue causes mental processes to be slowed down. A tired discus thrower won't set any new records. Good *physical condition* is another requirement of the outstanding athlete. One of the greatest thrills in sports must be to win the mile and still feel strong enough to take another lap. Fine athletes have shortened their careers by improper training. Unsteady legs and low stamina have no place in strenuous athletics.

Confidence is developed through steady, concentrated efforts to perform correctly. The athlete who doesn't believe in himself is a pushover. Overconfidence marks an untried and unpracticed would-be player. The degree of confidence needed comes from hours on the practice field or court. You know you can shoot, block, run, throw, hit, and perform other fundamentals required of good players.

Sometimes a group of fine athletes does not develop into a good team. The best players in the world will fail to win if they don't work together. Knowledge of teammates and their playing habits is gained only after long hours spent in the practice area. *Team work* will often overcome physical deficiencies such as short height, lack of speed or strength. Such team work is another reason why practice is well worth the effort and time it consumes.

There are many answers to the question, why practice? Good practice leads to automatic performance of fundamentals. It helps the athlete attain a high degree of stamina and body strength, which is essential for championship performances. Confidence and poise, the marks of an experienced athlete, are developed. Team effort is united. Brain as well as brawn is applied to the game. The thrill of scoring happens more often. So-called athletic "staleness" will not occur. Good practice makes great athletes; it makes champions.

Plan Your Daily Practice

Well-planned, detailed practice sessions are a necessity. Many coaches assume that having a practice schedule fixed in mind is adequate. However, the best returns on your effort are obtained by putting these plans on paper. Situations often arise during the course of a practice that may cause the coach to forget one of the most important parts of his mentally fixed practice schedule. To write his schedule would require only a few more minutes, and the insurance that a written plan provides is well worth the short amount of extra time.

Observe a good track team during its practice session. The coach has given the performers exact information concerning every minute of time to be consumed. He has a typed schedule that each boy studies. Watch the swimming instructor and his class. They move from one drill to another with a minimum of wasted time. These same conditions exist anywhere that good instruction is being presented. Basketball coaches might well utilize such practices. Intelligent practice planning and winning go hand in hand. Look up the records of the winning schools and you will find the schools that have planned and organized practice sessions.

Here are some of the advantages you will enjoy if your daily and season schedules are planned in detail:

- Budgeted time brings greater dividends. Short drills that are well presented cause more learning to occur than longer drills that often turn into drudgery. Players tend to "pace" themselves during long sessions. Obviously, this pacing develops bad habits.
- The environment of planned practice is conducive to good learning. The informality of athletics is tempered by the formality of good teaching techniques.
- The principle of continuous and progressive development is

exploited. This means that the team moves smoothly from the learned to the unlearned. A relationship exists between all drills.

● Players display high spirits and good morale, for knowledge dispels uncertainty. After a period of time the boys develop confidence in themselves and their coach.

● Your team gives an alert response to instruction. They believe in you. They *know* you are working, they *know* you are prepared. They *know* you are not depending on luck.

You will need two separate practice schedules. A daily plan and one covering the entire season are required. The season schedule is adjusted to your game dates. It will show all those tactical situations for which good basketball players must be prepared. Your daily plan consists primarily of fundamentals.

Gradually work the tactical situations into practices. Of course, we cannot practice all of these every day. This is another reason why practice plans are necessary. Records of each practice are kept. By checking them it is possible to determine quickly what has been neglected. Each situation needs to be practiced more than once. In some areas much time should be spent on offense against a zone defense. In other regions the teams are mostly strong set style teams. Work this out while considering your particular opponents.

Some tactical situations that will go in the season schedule are zone, man-for-man, pressing and combination zone-man-for-man defenses. Your own defenses against set style, "cat and mouse," free style, and fast break teams will need to be practiced. Offensive patterns, free throw, jump ball, and out of bounds situations need attention. The list can go on and on. Plan specific days to fit each into the daily workout.

What are the fundamentals you want your players to rehearse every day? Shooting, passing, rebounding, tip-ins, defense, and dribbling will certainly be included. Are there tactical situations that should be included in the every day practice? Let's add jump ball and out of bounds plays to the list.

Careful consideration should be given to your selection of drills. Drills should be designed for a specific purpose. Decide what your team needs and drills will be more wisely selected. They should actually comprise a part of your offense or defense in many cases. At other times it is necessary to work on a specific fundamental simply to develop that fundamental rather than to develop a part of your offense. The team using a single post will rarely have use for drills designed to develop pivot ability in the corner. The drills should be directly related to your offense.

When possible, use drills that develop more than one quality. A practice schedule composed of single purpose drills that is also a comprehensive schedule would take five hours to run. Youngsters must learn the relationship of the various parts of the game, and need practice at putting these parts together. Many boys are developed mechanically who can shoot well, dribble or pass well, but they have never learned how these skills are put together for the best results.

From the daily practice list, season practice list and a drills list, you are ready to draw up the daily practice. The following is a suggested plan for either high school or college, to be used prior to the first game:

```
 5 min............warm-up
25 min............set shooting
10 min............free throw shooting
 3 min............jump ball drill
 3 min............dribbling
 3 min............rebounding
 6 min............passing
              Drill 1
              Drill 2
 3 min............tip-in work
10 min............defensive workout
              Drill 1
              Drill 2
 5 min............rest period
15 min............offensive pattern
 6 min............system against press
 5 min............out of bounds plays
```

This practice runs for one hour and thirty-nine minutes. It is difficult to keep player interest alive for a longer period. Less time will suffice on certain days. The time element is flexible. Generally we can say that long drills tend to become monotonous and short ones are spirited and alert. Most coaches agree that more learning results from five minutes of practice each day for five days than twenty-five minutes in one day.

More skill is acquired when all basket shooting is done during a separate session devoted entirely to shooting. The entire afternoon session is then left for other practice. Basket shooting is time consuming. Coaches are aware of its absolute necessity. An hour is really needed. It is impossible to schedule an hour if your entire workout is conducted at one meeting.

No time is alloted for scrimmage in this practice plan. Scrimmage is overworked. Of course, *some* full court game type competition is essential. To enter a game without having had the benefit of several game-like scrimmage sessions would be suicidal. However, scrimmaging each day is just as unwise. Coach Paul Brown has said, "The coach who scrimmages every day cannot teach."

A rest period follows defensive work. Defensive work is most fatiguing when approached as a separate fundamental. It should be fatiguing, under all circumstances. Possibly 15 minutes of offensive practice is more than enough. If so, the players' attitude will serve as a gauge. Try to quit while the boys are still eager.

One of the tactical situations from the season schedule appears on this plan. Six minutes is not sufficient preparation for a pressing team. Practice against the press will occur on several other occasions. Rebounding and tip-in work are separated. The players are thus given an opportunity to regain leg strength.

Out of bounds plays have proved to be good drills on which to end the session. Run in alternating teams, the boys cool off slowly. Most players like to run these drills because much ball handling is involved. Much cutting and screening occurs that creates a good "team" feeling. Players should leave the court in such a frame of mind. Never let them leave in a listless manner. A number of efforts will help achieve this aim: for instance, music makes practice enjoyable for some boys. One manager will be pleased to operate the record player. Other than producing pep among the performers, music will bring rhythm and smoothness to their performances. Short drills, clean equipment, competition, and a good attitude among starters also help. At basketball practice we can use to advantage techniques that are employed in the classroom. Coaches are sometimes accused of being poor academic teachers. If this is true we are probably poor coaches.

Broken into elementary phases, basketball appears to be an elementary game. It becomes complex only when we realize that there are hundreds of these simple parts with which to be concerned. Basketball is still an infant in the sports world. The game is less than one hundred years old, but it is growing at a tremendous rate. Last year's game is out of date. Yesterday's methods must be adapted to the needs of today. Constant work is necessary in this as in no other sport if we are to compete successfully.

In the diagrams which accompany the drills discussed in the chapters that follow, the symbols used include:

————— Movement of player on floor
– – – – – – → Pass
• • • • • • • • Shot at basket or backboard
〜〜〜〜〜 Dribble
ıııı Handoff or soft pass, or tap
⌒⌒⌒⌒⌒ Rolling ball

3

Before-game Warm-up Drills

The amount of emphasis placed on the basketball pre-game ritual has varied so much with different teams and coaches that two distinct methods have evolved. One group wants the warm-up to reveal as little as possible the real strength of the team, and in doing so to appear drab and colorless. This team saves its potential strength for the actual competition. Another group would have its teams appear at their best even in the warm-up. These teams would be dressed nicely and look well drilled. They would look organized as soon as they appear on the playing floor. The majority of coaches probably follow some approach lying between these trends.

Before determining its importance, let's consider first the reasons for having a warm-up. One purpose is purely physical in nature. The athlete is rare who can perform his best without bending and stretching his muscles so that they become loose and supple. There is a possibility of pulled muscles resulting from a poor warm-up. How many times do we see inaccurate passes or missed lay-ups in the early minutes of the game? Most of these errors are due to improper warm-up.

Another reason for the warm-up that coaches are quick to point out is its tactical value. The warm-up period provides us with an opportunity to rehearse some of the plays and drills that are a part of our over-all offensive pattern shortly before the competition arrives. Some teams actually run their plays, if they use set plays, just before the game. Other coaches feel that the time required to perfect a drill of this type could well be spent on basket shooting, or performing some other skill that they feel is more important. A good pre-game drill will include sharp passing, some dribbling and lay-ups, pivoting, and rebounding. When several fundamentals are included in a warm-up drill, time will not be wasted if attention is given to the drill each practice session. The warm-up period should help the team become acquainted with possible differences in size and resiliency of the floor, distance of the basket from the wall, and other factors of this sort.

One function of the pre-game routine that we cannot overlook is its psychological aspect. The effect of seeing a finely organized team is sometimes detrimental to the opponent's morale. The strength of this effect will vary accordingly with the organization and skill of that opponent. Certainly, if well executed, the warm-up drill will develop confidence and good morale for any team. It will help develop the philosophy, "The best way to do is to be."

A player was once heard remarking humorously to his coach, "We didn't win all our games but we wore them out during warm-up period." This sums up the desirable player attitude rather well. Such players feel that even though they don't have a team with championship talent every year, they can always have a team that looks organized. They know they can have a team that does its best to make the trip worthwhile for its fans every time beginning with its appearance on the floor. Pride and confidence will be instilled in the conscientious player. Such drills will be an indication to all that this team is a *team* and as such has worked hard to reach that status.

1. Single Line Lay-up

The single line is often used as a sort of follow-the-leader drill to practice lay-ups from all angles of approach to the basket.

Procedure:

(a) All of the team members fall in a single line except one man, who stands under the goal.

(b) The first man dribbles in for a lay-up. The man under the goal retrieves the rebound and passes to the second man in line. The passer then goes to the end of the line and the shooter takes his place.

(c) The drill continues thus until all have shot. The leader then moves to a new starting position.

(d) This drill can be run by having two lines participate: one to dribble and lay-up and one to rebound and pass, with each performer exchanging lines.

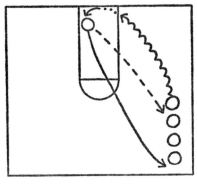

Diagram 1

2. Double Line Lay-up

This drill is probably the oldest warm-up drill in basketball. It is still a good one because it is quickly learned and has continuous movement.

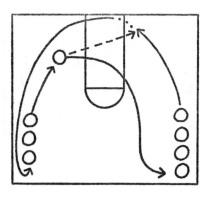

Diagram 2

Procedure:

(a) Half of the squad lines up on the sideline at center court with the other half of the team on the other sideline.

(b) The first man in the left line passes to the first man in the right line, as the right-hand man cuts in for a lay-up.

(c) Each succeeding man in line moves up to take the ball to pass or to receive. Run the drill to either side of the basket.

3. *Three Line Lay-up*

This drill adds one movement to the double line drill. The middle man performs a pivot before passing to the shooter. It is well suited to large squads where it is necessary to involve many players in one drill.

Procedure:

(a) Place one line of players behind the right sideline at center court. Another line is stationed behind the free throw line facing the goal. The third line is on the left side of the basket, facing the goal and ten feet away.

(b) The first man in the left line passes to the first man in the middle file at the free throw line. The receiver pivots backward and hits the first cutter from the right file for a lay-up shot.

(c) All men exchange lines from left to right. Run the drill both ways before discontinuing.

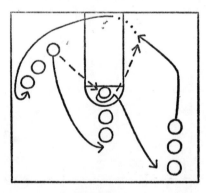

Diagram 3

4. *Figure Eight*

The figure eight can be adapted for use in many phases of basketball. During the warm-up it can be used most profitably.

Procedure:

(a) Station three lines at center court facing a basket. One line is on either sideline and the other is behind center circle. Each line is numbered.

(b) #2 starts the drill by passing to his right and cutting behind that receiver who is breaking for the pass.

(c) The receiver continues to move while he passes to #1 cutting from the left line. This player then passes to #2, the first ball handler, #2 shoots the lay-up.

(d) All three men can then take a lay-up as a good option for this drill. To perform the option, #1 retrieves the ball and passes to #3 breaking for a left hand lay-up. The original shooter retrieves the ball and passes to #1 as he cuts for a left hand lay-up. #3 will retrieve the ball and pass to #2, the original shooter, for another lay-up from the left side.

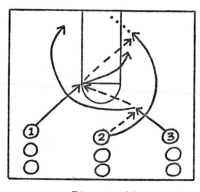
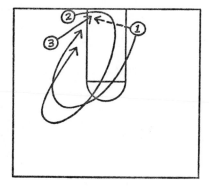

Diagram 4A   *Diagram 4B*

5. Single Line Pass, Pivot, Rebound and Lay-up

Here is a drill which incorporates nearly all of the fundamental skills.

Procedure:

(a) Station the men as shown in Diagram 5.

(b) #1 passes to #2. #2 passes to #3, who pivots and bounce passes to #4 cutting for the right hand lay-up.

(c) #1 takes #3's place, #2 takes #1's place and #3 goes to the end of the line. #4 takes #2's place. This means that #2 will pass to #4 who passes to #1 who passes to #5 as the cutter. The players

continue to shift in this manner as the drill is performed. It should
be worked also to the left side of the floor.

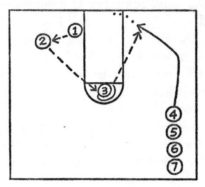

Diagram 5

6. *Side Post Drill*

Some drills are well suited to actual offensive patterns. The
side post drill is run by almost every single post team.

Procedure:

(a) Place the team in position as shown by Diagram 6.

(b) #1 passes to #2. #2 passes to #3 and breaks inside between
#3 and #4. #3 passes behind #2's back to #4 and follows the pass.
#1 fakes left and drives around behind #3 and off #4's left hip.
#4 may pass to #3 or #1. #1 and #2, who are guards, will exchange

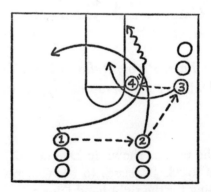

Diagram 6

lines. #3, a forward, and #4, a pivot man, each return to the same
line.

7. Two Line Trailer Drill

This drill offers action to a large number of boys. It is a better drill than the regular double line drill for that reason.

Procedure:

(a) Station the team in position as the diagram shows.

(b) The first man in the left line passes to the first man in the right line for a lay-up. The second man in the right file follows the shooter and retrieves the ball. He then passes to #1 three paces from the basket on the base line. #1 passes to #3 cutting for the lay-up on the left side. #4 follows, retrieves the ball and passes to #3 about three paces from the goal along the base line. #3 then passes to #5 cutting, and the drill moves continuously in this fashion.

(c) All players change lines after each performance.

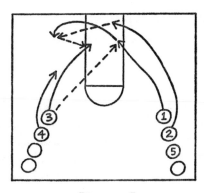

Diagram 7

8. Trailer Tip-in Drill

The tip-in is practiced during this drill in a rather unique manner.

Procedure:

(a) A single file is formed at center court.

(b) The first man dribbles to the basket and jumps as if to shoot a lay-up, but instead flips a soft pass in front of the rim.

(c) The second man in line is trailing him and goes up to tip the ball in the basket. The first man retrieves the ball and passes back to the third and fourth men, who perform in the same manner.

(d) Players should alternate as tippers and passers by changing their positions in line.

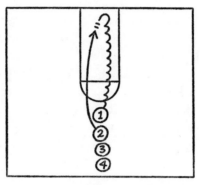

Diagram 8

9. *Four Corner Warm-up Drill*

Passing, timing and lay-ups from either side are featured in this drill.

Procedure:

(a) Place a line of players in each corner of a half-court.

(b) #1 starts the drill by passing to #4. #1 then takes his place at the end of that line. #4 passes to #2 and takes his place at the end of #2's line. #2 passes to #3 who is breaking across and down the middle for a right hand lay-up. #2 takes his place at the end of

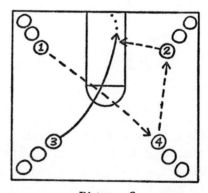

Diagram 9

line 3. #3 retrieves his own shot, passes to line 1 and goes to the end of line 1.

10. Pivot Drill

This drill gives the pivot ample opportunity to work in the post area prior to competition. It also gives all team members the chance to shoot lay-ups from all angles.

Procedure:

(a) Place the pivot man on the free throw line and all other players except #2 in one line as shown by the diagram.

(b) #1 starts the drill by passing to #2. #2 passes to the pivot man who hands off to #3 cutting off the pivot's right hip.

(c) #1 moves to #2's spot. #2 goes to the end of the line. The pivot retrieves the ball and passes to #4 who has taken #1's place and the drill continues.

(d) #3 returns to the same line.

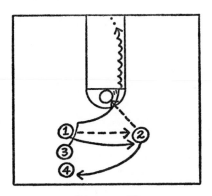

Diagram 10

11. Cutting Warm-up Drill

A lot of passing, timing, and cutting are involved in this drill. Teams using the double post will possibly like it best.

Procedure:

(a) Line the squad up in three lines at center court.

(b) #1 passes to #3 who passes to #2 cutting for the right hand lay-up.

(c) #1 retrieves the rebound and passes to #3 in the corner. #3 passes out to the second man in the middle line so that the drill can continue. The drill can be run in the opposite direction.

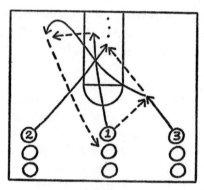

Diagram 11

Advanced Warm-up Drill

The following six drills are complicated and involved. They should not be attempted by weak teams or players who are not fundamentally sound. The results of such an attempt by unskilled players would be ludicrous. Senior high school teams or college teams who are sufficiently skilled will like the challenge and novelty offered by these drills.

12. Stetson Drill

This drill is quite involved and each player must be alert at all times.

Procedure:

(a) An even number of men are placed in the right line. Six is the minimum number for this line. Half the number of the right line is placed in the left line.

(b) #1 dribbles to the edge of the key hole area and pivots for a left hand flip pass to #2, who is breaking right behind him for the lay-up. #2 goes on under after the shot and halts three paces down the baseline to await the pass from #1. #1 retrieves, passes to #2, and returns to the end of the right line.

(c) #2 passes to #7 breaking for the left hand lay-up. #7 goes on under after the shot and halts three paces down the baseline.

#2 retrieves the ball, passes to #7 and takes his place at the end of the left line. #7 passes back to #3, who starts the drill over again involving three different men.

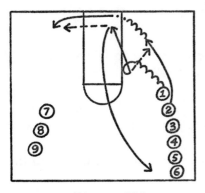

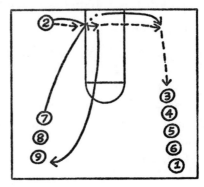

Diagram 12A   Diagram 12B

13. Five Man Continuity Drill

This drill moves very fast and requires sharp passing and good timing.

Procedure:

(a) Arrange the players on the floor as shown in Diagram 13.

(b) #1 passes to #2 and cuts off #5's left hip. #2 passes the ball in front of cutting #1's face and the pass is received by #5. #2 then cuts off #5's right hip.

(c) While this action is taking place, #3 and #4 are moving up to take #1 and #2's places.

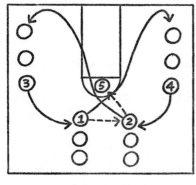

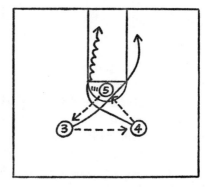

Diagram 13A   Diagram 13B

(d) #5 passes to #3. #3 passes to #4, #4 passes to #5 and #3 and and #4 criss-cross off #5, who can hand to either one of them.

14. Western Warm-up Drill

This drill is also quite involved.

Procedure:

(a) Station the team in position as shown on Diagram 14.

(b) #1 starts the drill by passing to #2. #2 passes to #4, and #4 passes to #3, who is cutting for the lay-up.

(c) #1 goes to the end of the outside line. #2 takes #1's place. #3 takes #4's place. #4 rebounds and goes to the end of the inside line.

(d) To practice left hand lay-ups the drill must be run to the other side of the floor.

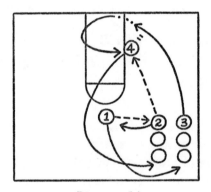

Diagram 14

15. St. Louis Warm-up Drill

One of the most colorful warm-ups, this drill should be attempted only by the most skilled players.

Procedure:

(a) Station the team members in their positions as shown by the diagram.

(b) #5 starts the drill by passing to #4. #4 passes to #1 and breaks between #3 and #1. #1 passes to #3 in front of the breaking #4. #3 follows his pass.

(c) #4 takes the pass from #3 and dribbles to the side of the basket where he goes up for a lay-up over the side of the rim; but at the last second he lays the ball back over his head in a soft delaying manner. #1 has made his turn and comes in at this time to go up and tip the ball back over his head softly to #2 (after receiving from #4). #2 tips back to #3 who tips to #4 coming in from the front. #4 tips back to #5. This man should be a great jumper and tipper. He tips the ball in the basket.

(d) A new group of five will then take a turn at the drill.

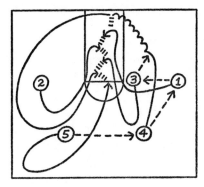

Diagram 15

16. Double Post Warm-up Drill

This drill has to be timed to avoid players colliding under the goal. It is a way of practicing the side post play on both sides at the same time.

Procedure:

(a) Place all guards in the two outside lines and all forwards in the corner lines as shown in the diagram. The post men will obviously be the best men for that position.

(b) #1 passes to #2 and breaks on his outside. #2 passes to #3 and follows off #3's left hip. #3 fakes to #2 and hits #1 for a left hand lay-up.

(c) At the same time this action takes place #4, using a second ball on the right hand side of the floor, passes to #5. #5 passes to #6 and follows the pass. #4 breaks outside #5 for the basket. #6 hands to #5, who swings on in for a left hand lay-up right behind #1.

(d) Many options can be used but this one will avoid collisions under the goal. To vary the drill have #3 give to #2 and #6 give to #4. In this way both are shooting lay-ups on the same side of the goal and will necessarily have to follow each other rather than collide.

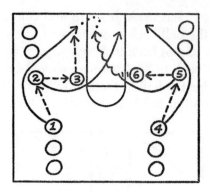

Diagram 16

17. *Two Ball Drill*

This drill is colorful. It is necessary to time the cut of each man perfectly to avoid confusion in the key hole area.

Procedure:

(a) Place two pivot men in the key hole, one on either side of the lane.

(b) Place all other players in two lines at center line.

(c) The first man in each line dribbles to the side line, stops and passes to the pivot man on his side. From here they each cut through the lane with the man from the left file going first.

(d) You will notice that #3 passes to the cutter from the opposite side of the floor, who is #2. #4 passes to the opposite cutter, #1.

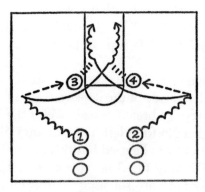

Diagram 17

Part II

DRILLS FOR TEACHING OFFENSIVE FUNDAMENTALS

"Doing a thing nearly right and doing it exactly right is usually the difference between failure and success." This statement could never be more true than when related to the teaching of offensive basketball fundamentals.

We are not going to list these skills in any manner that would indicate their degree of importance to the game. They are somewhat like the limbs of our body in that we would be greatly handicapped by the loss of any of them. For purposes of study and organization we shall call these fundamentals shooting, passing, dribbling, pivoting, rebounding, and tipping. Ball handling skills can and will be developed by the use of drills taken from any of these lists. Other than the fundamental categories it is necessary to add three other sections so that this offensive fundamental drills part will be complete. They are combination drills, fast break drills, and two and three man scoring drills.

4

Shooting Drills

Shooting is probably the easiest skill to develop, and therefore we shall start with its related drills. Youngsters want to work on shooting more than anything else for obvious reasons. Some present day players of wide fame and renown are such good shots that they have received the questionably complimentary title of "gunners." This title usually has a derogatory connotation, one that quite often distorts the facts. Present-day shooters are simply better shooters and future players are going to be even better. Coaches no longer assume that shooting is always a natural skill or one with which a boy is born. They have recognized the fact that satisfactory shooting can be *taught* and consequently a number of good drills have been created.

We shall divide shooting into three categories: lay-up, jump, and set shot drills.

I. Lay-up Shooting Drills

The lay-up is the most maltreated skill in basketball. Many youngsters have reached the erroneous conclusion that the only good lay-up is the jackknife twist with a half gainer shot. They feel that since it is supposed to be an easy shot the only way to look good on it is to make it tougher. The people who hold this view are wrong on both counts. First of all the lay-up *is* a very tough shot. Secondly, the most beautiful lay-up is an orthodox one with a strong high jump.

The lay-up is a tough shot to make because every time it is used, the shooter is coming in at a different angle and at a different speed. Usually there is an opponent who is trying to cram the ball down the shooter's throat. It is necessary to release the ball gently and yet the player is moving at a high rate of speed in most instances. So the very first requirement for shooting good lay-ups is to eliminate all unnecessary movements that are designed simply to look *pretty*.

The lay-up shot should be a high jump rather than a broad jump. The body momentum must be transferred upward and not outward. To achieve this, stretch on the last stride as the take-off foot is planted and lift the jumping leg hard, with the knee coming up high.

Protect the ball from opponents while shooting. Usually this means shooting the ball with the right hand on the right side of the goal and with the left hand on the left side of the goal. There are exceptions to this rule. The extremely flat drive down the baseline with the right hand makes it necessary to come up on the far or left side of the basket with a right hand lay-up; or, to shoot a left hand lay-up on the right side. When shooting the regular right hand lay-up on the right side of the goal, carry the ball well over to the right side of the body and keep the left hand between the ball and the opponent as the final thrust is given the ball by the right hand.

Aim the basketball. It is impossible to say just how many inches above the rim or what spot on the board to strike. This is impossible because of the different angles and speeds of the shot. Generally, it will be a spot about eight to twelve inches above the rim of the goal. The most important thing is to look up and to concentrate on the shot. It is then possible to judge the best point of impact between the ball and the backboard.

Shoot every lay-up off the boards whenever possible. Coaches vary in their opinions on this matter. No statistics are available to support my stand in this, but it appears to me that shots that are made too hard or too soft are helped by the board. Shooting against the board seems to allow for more error in judgment of speed than does the shot laid just over the rim, which has to be perfect.

In summation, here are the major things to look for in teaching the lay-up:

- Eliminate all fancy motions designed to look pretty.
- Lengthen the last stride and plant the take-off foot firmly.
- Transfer the body momentum upward rather than outward.
- Protect the ball from the opponent while the shot is being made.
- Aim the shot rather than throwing it up against the boards at random.
- Use the boards on every shot whenever it is possible to do so.

1. *High Jump Drill*

This drill is designed to encourage players to get up as high as possible for the lay-up instead of broad jumping.

Procedure:

(a) Place a chair slightly behind the backboard. Distance will depend upon the speed of the drill, which should be varied. For moderate speed put the chair directly under the board as in Diagram 1a. Put the chair back a yard for a fast drill, as in Diagram 1b.

(b) The coach should make the pass to each player as he approaches to make sure he does not veer to miss the chair. Encourage him to go straight for the chair and jump high so that he will come down on the floor in front of the chair instead of hitting.

(c) Use only one line and be sure to work from all angles.

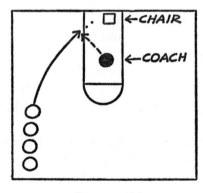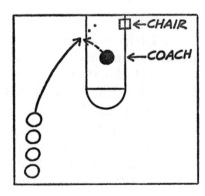

Diagram 1A	Diagram 1B

2. *Fake and Drive Drill*

This drill will help keep the defensive man off balance.

Procedure:

(a) Place each player in his offensive spot on the floor according to his playing position in actual game situations.

(b) Have managers place a chair in front of each boy.

(c) Utilize both ends of the floor. Have each boy fake alternately left and then right with a head, shoulder and foot fake before driving for the basket and a lay-up.

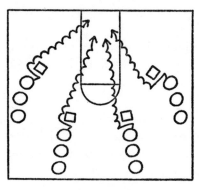

Diagram 2

3. *Competitive Lay-up Drill*

Youngsters should be encouraged to "make haste slowly" while performing this drill. Invariably the line that relaxes and makes every shot will be the line that wins.

Procedure:

(a) Divide the team into two equal teams and place one team at each end in a line facing the basket.

(b) Put the starting player in each line exactly the same distance from the basket he is facing.

(c) On a signal, the first player in each line breaks for the basket and a lay-up.

(d) As soon as he scores, and he should get it in the goal before quitting, he passes back to the second man in line. The second man may not leave the starting line until the ball touches his hands.

(e) This continues until one line has scored twenty points, with each goal counting two points.

(f) The lines should shout out their scores of the moment. For instance, if the first man scores, all members of his line should shout, "two!"

(g) Change the angle of approach to the basket frequently.

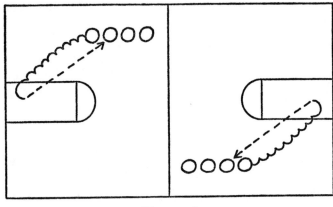

Diagram 3

4. Drill to Teach Firm Control of the Ball While Going up for a Shot

Many players will lose the ball if bumped only slightly on the shot. This costs them many points and, if the referee doesn't see it, possibly the ball. The following drill should instill the habit of firm ball handling on lay-ups.

Procedure:

(a) Line up some of the players facing the basket from any angle. The angle should be changed frequently.

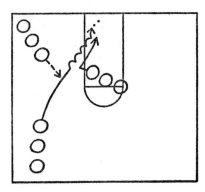

Diagram 4

(b) Another line of players stands near the goal.

(c) Players break for the basket one at a time, receiving a pass from a third line of players who stand closest to the goal.

(d) After the player receives the pass and starts up for the shot, the first man in the defensive line should push, bump, or hack him.

5. *Drill to Detect Open Man on Lay-up Drive*

Many players break for the basket like a runaway train. This is good *if* they can spot teammates who may be in better scoring position.

Procedure:

(a) Place two players near the basket with one on each side of the goal.

(b) Place a manager by each boy on the inside nearer the basket.

(c) Teach the managers certain hand signals (by use of fingers, arm positions, etc.) that will indicate when you want one of them to move quickly out to poor defensive position, leaving his man open, when you want both of them to move and when you want neither of them to move.

(d) A line of remaining players should be placed some good distance from the basket so that each in turn can dribble for the lay-up if neither teammate should suddenly be open.

(e) Vary the signals to the managers so that the players will have to adjust constantly to continuation of the drive or a pass off.

(f) Vary the angle of drive often.

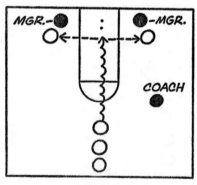

Diagram 5

6. *Drill to Teach Players to Cut Defensive Man Out Completely if They Have Half a Step Advantage*

This drill will show players that responsibility for contact is placed on defensive players when an offensive man has gained the advantage on a drive.

Procedure:

(a) Line the players up in two lines, one in the corner and one behind the right forward spot. The corner line is defensive.

(b) The first offensive man gets half a step ahead of the first defensive man.

(c) One the signal "go," the offensive player breaks across and toward the basket through the pivot area.

(d) A manager will pass to the offensive player after he takes one or two strides.

(e) The offensive player then swings in and cuts *out* the defensive man. He goes for a left hand lay-up on the far side of the basket.

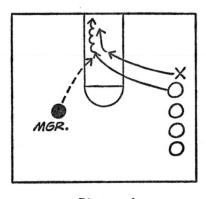

Diagram 6

7. *Drilling Players to Veer Enough for Shooting a Lay-up Off the Backboard When Coming Straight Down the Middle*

Quite a few coaches want their players to use the board on all lay-ups. Some coaches do not have a preference but merely want to see the ball go in the hole. If a coach has a preference, this drill should develop the desired habit in his players.

Procedure:

(a) Place a chair directly under the goal.

(b) Line up the players in the middle of the floor, directly under the basket.

(c) As each player breaks in turn for the basket, toss him a pass on the free throw line.

(d) He will then take a dribble and adjust to the chair by going to one side or the other so that a shot can be banked off of the boards.

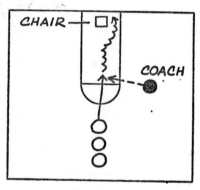

Diagram 7

II.   Jump Shooting Drills

It has been said many times recently that the jump shot is changing our entire concept of basketball. Statistics seem to bear out the truth of this statement. Watch any game, whether high school, college, or recreation league and you will almost certainly see the majority of points scored on jumps.

The jump shot increases the value of the boy with good strong legs and an ability to jump. Although some good jump shooters don't get up very high but rely on quickness of the jump, most coaches prefer a good high jump. The height of the jump lessens the chances that the shot will be blocked.

The jump shot should be a set shot from a higher position for the one-handed shooter. It should not be a strenuous, jerky motion. The jump shot should be a smooth, easy, elevated set shot with a good follow through. To accomplish this, don't try to shoot the ball from behind the head. Don't bend backwards.

Hunch the shoulders forward and position the ball in front of the face and above the head with arms slightly flexed. The right hand does the work, while the left hand balances the ball for the right-hand shooter. Feet should be spread slightly and many boys find it more comfortable to slide one of them slightly forward as in the position for the old two hand set shot.

Do not try to *guide* the ball. Shoot the basketball. By shooting, we mean relax and follow through. Attempts at guiding the ball cause one to tense up and follow through improperly.

Here are some points the coach should look for:

- A good strong jump.
- Ball position should be in front of and above the head so that the shooter may sight just under the ball.
- Keep the body balanced. Don't lean backwards. The shoulders should be on a line drawn upward from the hips or slightly inclined in front of the hips.
- Handle the ball gently and follow through. Handle it as if it were an egg that would break if handled roughly. This causes the shooter to shoot a "dead" or light ball instead of the heavy, hard shot that rebounds so strongly.
- Shoot the ball instead of *guiding* it.

8. *Drive and Jump Shot Drill*

The quick stop and jump shot is probably the most important offensive maneuver in basketball today. It is imperative that time be spent each day on this skill.

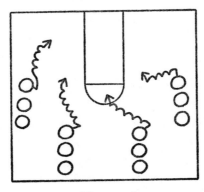

Diagram 8

Procedure:

(a) Place all of your players in their normal offensive positions.

(b) Have them drive for one or two dribbles to the left and stop quickly for a jump shot.

(c) After several minutes, have them drive to the right for a quick stop and jump shot.

(d) Let your pivot work for a short time in each line.

9. Practicing the Standing Jump Shot

Most boys can drive and jump very well because their momentum helps to get them up in the air. Few can jump really well from a flatfooted position. If the player does not practice to correct this, he is an incomplete basketball player.

Procedure:

(a) All players get in their normal offensive positions and then take two strides forward. If this does not place them close enough to the basket, arrange the distance in accordance with their jumping ability.

(b) Give each line a ball. Have them take turns retrieving and passing to their own line, where the receiver will immediately take a jump shot without dribbling.

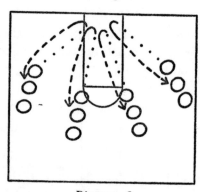

Diagram 9

10. Jump Shot Drill to Prevent Players from Traveling Too Far Forward Before Landing

Often boys get a habit of jumping and traveling forward to such an extent that they hit the defensive man if he is in good position. The following drill is designed to eliminate such a weakness.

Procedure:

(a) Place chairs in front of all lines. The lines should be arranged one behind each offensive position.

(b) The pivot may alternate lines.

(c) Let each player in turn drive and jump from a spot directly in front of the chair.

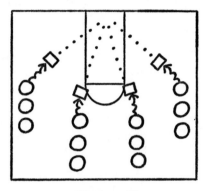

Diagram 10

11. *Quick Stop and Jump Shot Drill*

This drill will teach the basketball player the art of stopping while moving at high speed and to get his shot off on balance.

Procedure:

(a) Form three lines. One is placed under the basket to retrieve, one at a side position to pass to the cutting line that will come at varying angles.

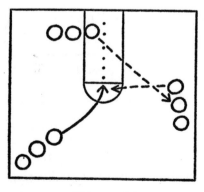

Diagram 11

(b) Let the passing line start by hitting the cutter at about the head of the circle as he breaks quickly for the basket. All three lines should rotate so that each boy at one time or another becomes a passer, a retriever, and a shooter.

12. *Jump Shot Over Low Man*

Many times a tall player will be close to the basket with a defensive man on him who is in good position. This defensive man will often be extremely close but in a low retreating position and even off balance to the rear. This is a time when the offensive player can jump without dribbling for an easy basket. This holds true on some occasions where the players are of equal height.

Procedure:

(a) Put one team of players in offensive position with all members having a ball. Put another team as defensive men in the low close defensive position already described.

(b) The offensive men attempt to get their shots off high and protect the ball as they bring it into shooting position.

(c) Allow the defensive men to knock the ball out of the offensive players' hands if they bring it too low when starting the jump.

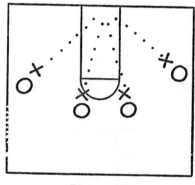

Diagram 12

III. Set Shooting Drills

There are as many good set shots as there are good basketball players. Because of physiological differences in structure of the hands, arms, and shoulder girdle, variations in form can be observed in good shooters who are actually trying to shoot alike.

However, adherence to certain fundamental rules will help no matter what style is used. Some outstanding shooters have such unorthodox shots, they appear to defy all conventions of good shooting. A closer look will usually prove that they follow at least three rules of good form: get on balance, aim, and follow through.

Some boys are actually on balance when they appear otherwise. Others could improve their shot by getting on balance. Remember, we are concerned with teaching the *best* procedures.

Aiming is a matter of concentrating as well as sighting. Some coaches advocate shooting just over the front rim. Others like to use the rear rim as an aiming point. We like to consider the *whole* basket as a circular black bullseye. The shooter takes a concentrated *sight picture* and attempts to strike the center of the target.

A follow through is essential to smooth, accurate shooting. It is an integral part of the two-hand set, the moving one hander, and the stationary one hander. Look for a full extension of the fingers and in the case of the one hander, a flexion of the wrist. The ankles will also be extended in the follow through.

As in the case of the jump shot, it is necessary to *shoot* the ball instead of *guiding* it. A sense of rhythm is helpful. Eliminate jerky motions that look mechanical. The shot should appear to consist of only one smooth, continuous motion.

Here are some instructional points to keep in mind:

- Body balance.
- Aiming. Considering the basket a bullseye. Take a good sight picture.
- Concentration. A shooter can almost "think" the ball in the basket.
- Follow through.
- Rhythm and smoothness of motion.

13. Set Shooting from Position

Each player should have a spot where he can hit most accurately if his defensive man shows him daylight. This spot might well be what we consider normal offensive position for the forwards and guards. The pivot can work on hooking from the spot where he most often receives the ball.

Procedure:

(a) Place each player in the spot where the coach wants him to play in a game.

(b) Place a defensive man on each shooter in such a position that the shooter can get his shot off—if he refuses to let the waving hand of the defensive boy annoy him.

(c) Let defensive and offensive men exchange places every five minutes.

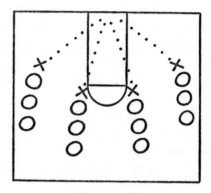

Diagram 13

14. *Around the World Drill*

Players like to have competition added to practice when it is possible. Proof of this is the fact that, left alone for free play, they will play games that are invariably competitive. "Around the World" is one such shooting game that they like.

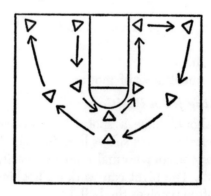

Diagram 14

Procedure:

(a) More than three players should not participate on one end of the floor. If the entire squad is to participate, several baskets are needed.

(b) The first shooter starts under the basket for an easy shot and continues to shoot from the spots designated in the diagram until he finishes or misses.

(c) If he misses, he can take a chance on hitting the second shot from where he missed and continue on. If he should miss this shot, he has to start from the beginning. He can choose to wait until it becomes his turn again and start from the spot where he missed.

15. *A Shooting Game Called "Golf"*

This is another of the games youngsters like to play when practicing unsupervised. If the school has an old gym or a practice gym it might be well to mark "holes" permanently on the floor. Team members could shoot at par in their spare time. Record the names and dates of each par shooter on the gym bulletin board.

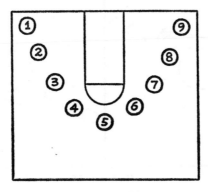

Diagram 15

Procedure:

(a) Mark with tape or paint the nine spots from which players are to shoot.

(b) Each shooter will start at the first hole and shoot until he makes the basket from that spot. He then moves to the second and so on until he completes the course.

(c) Only the total number of "strokes" is recorded. The player taking the fewest shots at the basket while scoring from each hole is the winner.

16. Competitive Set Shooting Drill

This drill will encourage boys to get their set shots off quickly. At the same time it emphasizes the need for concentration on the target and demonstrates the foolhardiness of just "throwing" the ball up there.

Procedure:

(a) Place a line at each end of the floor with each line being the same distance from the basket on its end of the gym.

(b) On a signal the first player shoots a set, retrieves the rebound and tosses back to the next player in line who has taken his place.

(c) When one line scores twenty with each goal counting two points, that line is declared the winner.

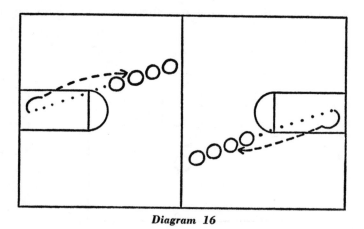

Diagram 16

IV. Free Throw Shooting Drills

Free throw rules have been revised almost yearly since Dr. Naismith's boys first tossed soccer balls at peach baskets. No matter how they are enforced, free throws continue to total a large percentage of point production. The free throw situation is strategic whether the shot is made or missed. We must be prepared to cope with *all* conditions that arise during a game. Free throw situations occur so often that they assume a degree of game control that many abhor. Nonetheless, every team has the same opportunity to cash in on this aspect of the game.

The secret to shooting free throws successfully may be explained in one word—practice. The style is of secondary importance. Generally, we say that a two-hand set shooter should shoot his free throws the same way. We say that a one-handed set shooter should shoot free throws with one hand. This rule is not hard and fast; the two-hand underhand method is also good and nobody shoots set shots that way nowadays.

No matter which style is used, the player can achieve a high degree of efficiency by shooting 100 free throws each day. The shooter should stand close to the line in a balanced stance. Have him step back and assume his stance again after each pair of shots.

An extra problem is attached to free throwing. Because of the signficance of the free throw point and audience attention, the shooter has difficulty in relaxing. To combat this problem, many coaches and players believe that a deep breath prior to the shot induces more relaxation. The professional stars have added strength to the belief. As a result, this deep inhalation has been dubbed by flippant high school players as the "television breath." Such an attitude will surely lessen its effectiveness. Used with the proper attitude, this deep breath procedure has some merit. Other methods or mannerisms that help the youngster to relax are possibly just as good.

We believe that the less waste motion a shooter employs, the less likelihood there is of his missing. The shot is short and requires little strength. A one-hand shooter needs no effort other than a hand, wrist, and ankle extension. He should start the shot high, requiring only the final push.

Some points of instruction for the coach to keep in mind are·

- The set shooting style of the free thrower.
- Stance.
- Relaxation.
- Elimination of waste motion
- Concentration and aiming.
- Follow through.

17. *Accuracy Drill*

The aim of this drill is to put as much game-type pressure on the shooter as possible.

Procedure:

(a) Place five men at each basket.

(b) Without a time limit, have each player shoot twice so that if everyone is accurate ten points will be scored at the end of one round.

(c) The winner is that group which has the most points.

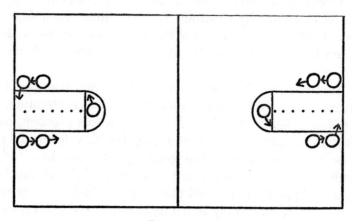

Diagram 17

18. *Competitive Free Throw Drill*

The purpose of this drill is to get players in the habit of reacting after every shot, whether it is made or missed.

Procedure:

(a) Station six men under a basket. In this drill #1 is the starting shooter. #1, #3 and #5 are on a team and #2, #4 and #6 are also a team.

(b) If #1 makes the shot, he keeps shooting until he has made five consecutive shots. At that time a teammate becomes the shooter. Any time he should miss, a teammate will become the shooter until all members of one team have had a turn. Then the three members of the other team take their turns in a like manner.

(c) When a shooter misses, his teammates try to make the tip-in. The opposing team tries to get possession and dribble out to the free throw line while the shooting team tries to prevent them. If the opposing team is successful in dribbling the ball out, they may become shooters in this way.

(d) Count each field goal or tip-in as two points and each free throw as one point. The game objective is twenty points.

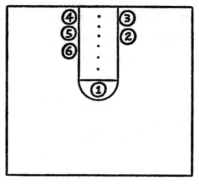

Diagram 18

19. *Free Throw Golf Game*

This game will not allow a player to get set at the goal so that his shots become mechanical. He must move from one goal to the other and take his position each time.

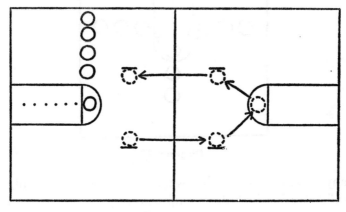

Diagram 19

Procedure:

(a) Start all players at one goal. Each player will shoot one time at that goal and move in a clockwise direction to the next goal. We are assuming here that most modern gyms will have four, six or more goals.

(b) After the team has shot at each goal, check to find out how many "par" shooters you have. Par will be that number of goals that the gym has.

20. Free Throw Distraction Drill

This drill is designed to put more pressure on the shooter. It should also teach him the importance of concentration.

Procedure:

(a) Place the squad in three lines, with one on the free throw line and one on either side.

(b) The first man in the middle line shoots two free throws while the first two men in the other two lines try to distract him by waving their arms and talking to him. They should not touch the shooter in any way.

(c) The performers will go to the ends of the lines, alternating from left to right. Three new men then take their places in the drill.

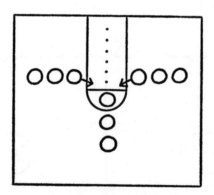

Diagram 20

Many good shooting drills, especially lay-ups, can be obtained from Chapter 3, which deals with warm-up drills.

5

Passing Drills

Passing is a composite skill. Peripheral vision, quick hands, good timing, and a keen intellect are usually qualities that produce outstanding passers. The simplest quality is probably the most important attribute a good passer must possess: he must be basically and inherently a *good team man*. Some players make seemingly good passes that are often intercepted. Even though the receiver must be alert and assume his share of responsibility, every passer should automatically begin wondering what he did wrong when his pass is incomplete.

We feel that proper use of drills will help to develop the desired qualities and habits in the boy who is genuinely interested in improving himself.

I. Passing Drills

1. *Five Star Drill*

The five star drill requires the individual to meet the pass, pass quickly and accurately, and then move to a new position. This drill is continuous and the player must be alert.

Procedure:

(a) Four men form a square ten feet apart with a fifth man placed in the middle.

(b) The middle man has the ball. He passes to any player and then takes his place.

(c) The receiver passes to either man on his right or left and takes his place.

(d) The second receiver passes across the square to the opposite corner man and takes his place.

(e) The third receiver passes to the man on his right or left and takes his place.

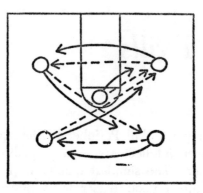

Diagram 1

(f) The drill continues in this manner with the ball moving across (corner to corner), a side pass, across, a side pass, etc.

(g) After the drill is well learned, a variation may be added. Each receiver fakes before passing.

2. *Circle Drill or Bull in the Ring*

Here is a drill that can be used as a defensive maneuver. The greatest results, however, are obtained from the passing practice

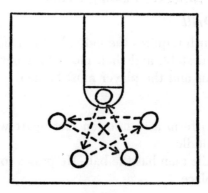

Diagram 2

involved. Consider the ball as a "hot" object that has to be moved quickly and accurately so that it will not burn.

Procedure:

(a) Form a circle with five men around the center circle area. Place a sixth man in the middle of this circle.

(b) The ball is passed by, around, or over this man who makes every effort to deflect or intercept the passes.

(c) The passer cannot pass to his right or left but must pass to one of the men across the circle from him.

(d) If the middle man intercepts or deflects a pass, the passer exchanges places with him.

3. Two Line Drill

This drill makes it a bit harder to pass by the defensive man who is squared away facing the offensive player. It can also be used as a defensive drill.

Procedure:

(a) Two files face each other with ten feet separating the first man in each file.

(b) One man stands in the middle between the two lines and faces the man who has the ball.

(c) The player who has the ball attempts to pass by the middle man to the first man in the opposite line.

(d) Whether the pass is successful or not, the passer takes the middle man's position. The middle man goes to the end of the line and the receiver then attempts to pass by the new middle man. The drill continues in this fashion.

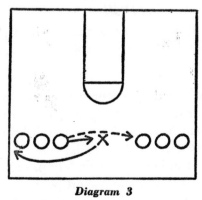

Diagram 3

4. *Follow the Leader*

Here is a drill that allows for practice of a variety of passes in simple formation. A maximum opportunity for the coach to make correction of poor passing form is offered.

Procedure:

(a) All players line up in one file. The first man is given a ball.

(b) This first player dribbles out two or three dribbles, turns and passes, using a hook, chest, bounce, or any kind of pass he chooses.

(c) Each member of the line will make the same type of pass as his turn arrives.

(d) When the leader's turn comes again, he uses another type of pass for all the others to imitate.

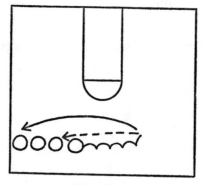

Diagram 4

5. *Four Corner Passing Drill*

Once learned, this drill enables an entire squad to practice passing with several types of passes being employed.

Procedure:

(a) Divide the squad into four groups and place a group at each corner of a half court, facing the free throw line.

(b) The first player in line 1 starts the drill by making a long pass to the first player in line 2 (see Diagram 5).

(c) The receiver in line 2 immediately passes back to the first player who advances rapidly for a short pass.

(d) As soon as the first player receives this return pass, he

comes to a halt and fires a pass to the first player in line 2, who
is breaking toward line 3.

(e) The first player from line 2 and the first player from line
3 go through the same procedure. The first player from line 3 and
the first player from line 4 then also go through the same routine.

(f) After the drill is well learned, put another ball into play.
Some squads can perform this drill successfully with four balls
in action.

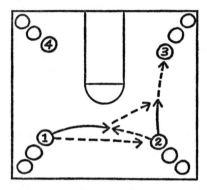

Diagram 5

6. *Taking Handoff and Passing at Top Speed*

Coaches who are strong believers in the "running game" will
like this drill.

Procedure:

(a) The squad can be divided into several groups. At least
three men should be in each group.

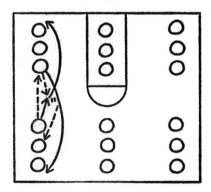

Diagram 6

(b) One method of running the drill is to arrange a formation with three lines facing three lines from a distance of ten feet.

(c) The first man in each line passes to the first man in the opposite line and breaks to a point halfway between the lines. The receiver then passes back to him and cuts fast for a hand-off. The player who takes the handoff passes immediately to the second man in the first line.

(d) Players change lines after they have performed.

7. A Drill for Practicing the Hook Pass

Hook passes are not used as often in today's game of basketball as in the early days of the game. There are still occasions when it is the logical pass to use, and its development should not be neglected.

Procedure:

(a) Split the squad into two groups. Place one group at the right forward spot and the other at the right guard position.

(b) Give the ball to the first man in the outside line. The first guard passes to the first man in the forward line, and cuts on his outside.

(c) The first forward hands off to the cutting guard and breaks for the basket across the keyhole, looking over his right shoulder for a hook pass from the guard.

(d) The forward should be able to go up for a left hand lay-up on the far side of the basket as soon as he receives the pass, without having to dribble.

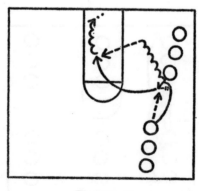

Diagram 7

(e) Vary the drill by running to the left side of the floor or by letting the forward fake to the cutting guard and swing a left hand hook to the guard as he approaches the basket.

8. *Two Lines Hook Passing*

Here is a drill that puts two balls into play with continuous hooking—practicing with one hand and the other.

Procedure:

(a) Form the squad into two files facing in the same direction, and about six feet apart.

(b) The first player in the right file dribbles out ten feet and hooks with the right hand to the second man in the left file.

(c) Meanwhile, the first man in the left file has dribbled out and is hooking to the second man in the right file.

(d) The passers then exchange lines.

(e) This drill could well be used to practice on a number of different types of passing.

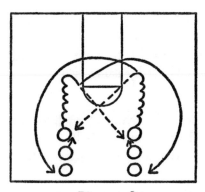

Diagram 8

9. *Lead Pass Drill*

The objective of this practice is to teach players to lead receivers, especially when they are breaking away from the passer.

Procedure:

(a) Four lines are needed, one in each corner of a half court.

(b) The first man in file 1 passes to the first player in file 2. The receiver flips the ball to the player standing directly behind him and breaks toward the third file.

(c) The cutting player receives a lead pass and immediately passes to the first man in file 3. This receiver flips the ball to the second man in file 3, and breaks hard toward file 4.

(d) The drill continues in this fashion around and around the half court area. After it is well learned by the team, two or three balls may be put into action.

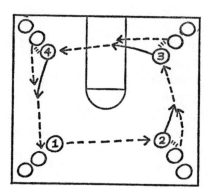

Diagram 9

10. *Diamond Passing Drill*

The purpose of this drill is to get a great deal of passing practice done in a short while by using two balls.

Procedure:

(a) Station a line of players at each corner of a half court.
(b) Give lines 1 and 3 each a ball.
(c) The players with a ball will pass to the first men on their

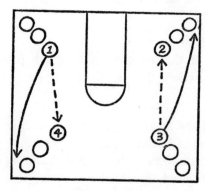

Diagram 10

right and take a position at the end of that line to which they have passed.

(d) After some time has elapsed, change the drill by having passes made to the left.

11. Speed and Competitive Passing

This is a drill to increase the pleasure players get from performing practice activities. It is also an excellent method of teaching speed passing.

Procedure:

(a) Divide the squad into two teams and place them in a circle, with every other one being on the same team.

(b) Place a member from each team in the center of the circle and give each a ball.

(c) On a signal from the coach, the middle men start passing to each of their teammates. The balls move in a clockwise direction around the ring:

(d) The middle men should start on opposite sides of the ring. Their objective is to overtake the other team.

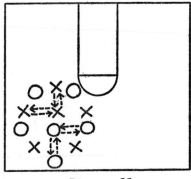

Diagram 11

12. Follow the Pass Drill

The objective of this drill is to instill the habit of moving after releasing the ball.

Procedure:

(a) The squad is divided into four groups and one group is stationed at each corner of a half court.

(b) The first man in line 1 passes to #2, who passes to #3,

who passes to #4. Each passer follows his own pass and takes a position at the end of the line to which he passes.

(c) The drill can be varied by having the passers break to the line opposite the one to which they have passed.

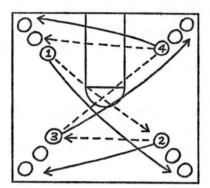

Diagram 12

13. *Double Circle Drill*

This is a short pass drill to teach players to "soften" passes when the receiver is standing close by.

Procedure:

(a) Station one circle of five men inside a circle of seven men.

(b) Two balls may be used. Start one on each side of the inner ring passing to the outer ring and receiving. Balls will be moved around the double circle in the same direction.

(c) Vary the length of distance between the inner and outer circle to practice different types of passes.

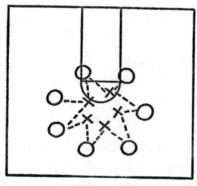

Diagram 13

14. *Pass Accuracy Drill*

The purpose of this drill is to add interest to passing practice and to develop keen accuracy.

Procedure:

(a) Using a rope, suspend a rubber tire from the ceiling or balcony so that it is five feet from the floor.

(b) Place two lines of players facing each other on each side of the tire and fifteen feet away from it.

(c) Give a ball to the first man in one of the lines and have him chest pass to the first man in the other line. The catch is that he must pass through the tire as it is swung by a manager. His pass must be timed to pass through the tire when it is between him and his receiver. The lines will alternate in passing in this manner.

Sketch for Drill #14. Pass Accuracy Drill.

15. *Speed Passing Drill*

The purpose here is to improve accuracy and speed. Many players can pass accurately as long as they are not hurried. Unfortunately most defensive players thwart any attempts to pass slowly.

Procedure:

(a) Station several lines of players along a wall, at the same distance from it.

(b) Each line should have a circle target drawn on the wall at chest height.

(c) Each player in turn attempts to make as many passes as possible strike the area within the circle during a thirty-second interval, which is timed by the coach.

16. *Halfcourt Passing Game*

By eliminating dribbling entirely, this drill causes more passing to occur and thereby affords the players an extra amount of time on ball handling.

Procedure:

(a) Divide the squad into groups of threes.

(b) Start six players on each end of the floor on a three on three game of passing and shooting only—no dribbling.

(c) If all of the squad is not active, allow those waiting to compete against the winners.

(d) Set a certain score as "game."

(e) Vary by allowing only left-handed passes and permit only left-handed lay-up shots to be made.

II. Post Passing Drills

17. *Two Ball Drill Especially for Pivot Men*

Although this drill is designed primarily for pivot men, it will improve the ability of all team members to feed the post man.

Procedure:

(a) Place all team members in lines at their offensive spots. All players should face the post man, who is stationed on the free throw line.

(b) Each guard has a ball. The left guard passes to the pivot, who passes quickly to the right forward.

(c) As soon as he can make a pass without ruining the continuity of the drill, the right guard passes to the post, who passes quickly to the left forward.

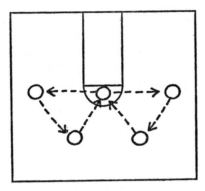

Diagram 17

(d) Forwards should pass back to the nearest guards immediately. The guards continue hitting the pivot and receiving a pass back from the forwards after the pivot has shoveled it to them. All types of effective passes should be employed.

18. Pepper the Post

Here is another drill to impress the pivot man with his responsibility for receiving passes well.

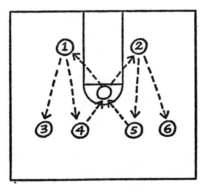

Diagram 18

Procedure:

(a) Break the squad into groups of seven, with one post man in each group.

(b) Line them up as shown in Diagram 18.

(c) Start with two balls being used and as skill increases a third ball may be added.

(d) Player #4 passes to the post man who passes quickly to #2. #5 then passes to the post man who passes quickly to #1. #1 can pass out to #3 or #4. #2 can pass out to #5 or #6. The front men who receive the passes from #1 and #2 immediately pass to the post, who has to get rid of the ball quickly and be ready for the next pass.

19. *Delayed Pivot Passing*

Often the pivot cannot make the pass to a guard when he is cutting off the post man's hip. On such occasions the pivot can wait until the guard has cleared, turn and hit him under the basket.

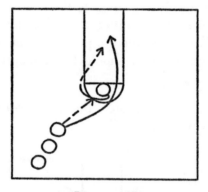

Diagram 19

Procedure:

(a) Station the post man anywhere in his area that will enable him to work as much as possible as he does in actual game situations.

(b) Form a line of players at one of the guard spots.

(c) The first player in line passes to the post man and cuts close by the post, continuing on toward the basket.

(d) The post man should fake to the cutter, pivot in the opposite direction and pass to the cutter under the goal, using a two-handed overhead pass.

(e) For variation have a player guard the post man. The post man should then have to make a decision to hand off as the cutter approaches him or delay and hit the cutter under the basket.

20. Hook Pass Drill for Forwards and Pivot

All forwards get caught occasionally on their drive down the base line and start looking for the post man.

Here is a drill to prepare for such occasions.

Procedure:

(a) Station men in four lines as indicated in Diagram 20.

(b) The first player in line 1 breaks with a dribble down the base line for a basket. The first player in line 3 breaks toward the free throw line and takes #1's hook pass.

(c) Player #3 turns for a left-hand hook pass to #4, who is breaking down the base line for the goal.

(d) #4 jumps immediately for a left hand hook to the player from line 2 who is breaking toward the free throw line.

(e) The player from line 2 immediately hooks with the right hand to a second cutter from line 1. The drill then moves continuously, with lines swapping as shown in the diagram.

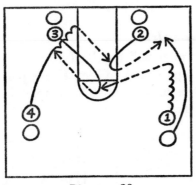

Diagram 20

21. Feed the Pivot Practice

Here is a drill that makes it mandatory for the post man to be agile and move around in order to get the ball in scoring territory.

Procedure:

(a) Form four lines facing the pivot area with the first man in line in possession of a ball.

(b) Put all the pivot men in one line under the goal behind the base line. Assign one man to guard the pivot who is participating.

(c) The first pivot breaks and maneuvers in the pivot area until he has received and passed back to every one of the men in the semi-circle.

(d) The second pivot man then attempts to maneuver in the same manner while the defensive man attempts to bat down or intercept the passes.

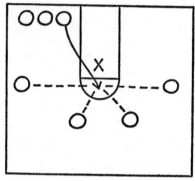

Diagram 21

22. *Pivot Passing Drill*

Often the post man will hand off to a cutter who runs into trouble and has to pass back to him. If this post man is not alert he will fumble the pass or miss it completely. Here is a drill to help eliminate such a possibility.

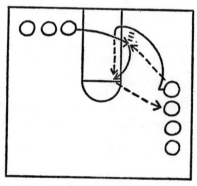

Diagram 22

Procedure:

(a) Place all post men under the goal and to one side of it behind the base line.

(b) All other players line up behind the right forward position.

(c) The first man in the post man's file breaks across the three-second area and will stop just outside of that zone.

(d) The first man in the outside line passes, fakes a cut to his left and breaks right off the pivot's left hip for a handoff.

(e) The outside man quickly passes back to the pivot, who fires a chest pass to the second man in the outside file.

(f) The drill begins again with two new men maneuvering. This drill should be run on both sides of the floor before discontinuing practice.

23. Passing to Pivot Over Face Guarding Defensive Player

If your post man is small, many opponents will try to play in front of him. This can be disastrous if your outside boys aren't adept passers. The best cure is an "ounce of prevention."

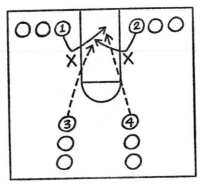

Diagram 23

Procedure:

(a) Place all players except the post men in two files behind the guard positions.

(b) Two lines of post men are formed as shown in Diagram 23.

(c) A ball is given to the first men in each outside file.

(d) The post man in line 1 breaks forward and cuts for the basket. A lead pass is given by the first man in line 4.

(e) The first post man in line 2 performs the same maneuver for a pass from file 3.

(f) Post men and outside men go to the end of the opposite line, but continue strictly as post men or as outside men.

24. *Peripheral Vision Drill for Post Men*

The purpose of this drill is to help post men develop the ability to see out of the corners of the eyes.

Procedure:

(a) All pivot men are stationed in one line behind the free throw line.

(b) All other players are stationed in two lines behind the offensive guard positions.

(c) Both front men in the outside lines have a ball. Each takes a turn at passing and receiving from the first post man. The outside boys gradually work around as far to the post man's side as he can see, receive passes, and function efficiently. When he misses he goes to the end of his own line and the outside boys go to the end of the opposite outside line.

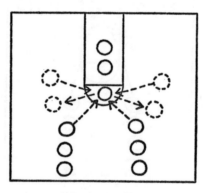

Diagram 24

III.   Receiving Drills

25. *Two Ball Split Vision Drill*

Modern basketball cannot be effective if passers "point" or "telegraph" their passes. Peripheral vision development is a must.

Procedure:

(a) Form one line of players in a company front formation, side by side. Not more than six or less than four should be in this line.

(b) One player is placed about eight feet from the middle man in the line and facing all the other players.

(c) The player facing the line and one member of the line are given balls.

(d) As the player facing the line passes to any member of the line, the other ball is passed to him. The two balls are then moved continuously from the line to the one man.

(e) Twenty to thirty seconds "out front" are sufficient. All participants should be given an opportunity to be the front man.

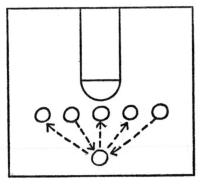

Diagram 25

26. *Drill for Teaching Flip Pass Handoff*

The handoff is often overlooked. It is also often taken for granted. The following drill will help to condition athletes physically and teach them the handoff pass.

Procedure:

(a) Place four chairs on one end of the floor in the positions shown in Diagram 26.

(b) One team of five men is then put in position with the ball in the hands of one of the front men.

(c) A shoulder-high flip pass is given the first receiver as the passer breaks hard down the floor.

(d) Each receiver flip passes as soon as the ball hits his hands

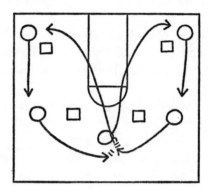

Diagram 26

and then breaks immediately so that he will get back in time for his next pass.

27. *Quick Adjustment Drill*

Here is a maneuver that teaches receivers to make quick adjustment even if the pass comes high, low or wide.

Procedure:

(a) Cut a steel drum down the middle from end to end so that two semi-circle sections are obtained. For your purposes only one section is needed, unless you wish to build two drill areas.

(b) Attach this section against a wall at waist height.

(c) Players line up facing the projecting semi-circle of the steel drum.

(d) The first player passes the ball against the drum and moves quickly out of the way as the second player receives the richocheting ball.

(e) The second player then makes a pass against the drum and the third player recovers the ball. The drill is continued so long as benefit is derived from it.

Sketch for Drill #27. Quick Adjustment Drill.

28. *Five Man Weave*

Five man weave is good for developing the ability to hand off accurately and without fumbling or losing possession of the ball.

Procedure:

(a) Arrange the squad into five lines at one end of the gymnasium.

(b) The middle man has the ball and starts the drill by handing off to player #4. #3 then goes behind #4 and #5 and prepares to cut and return across the floor for the pass and another handoff.

(c) As #4 receives the ball, he is cutting diagonally across the floor toward #2. #4 hands off to #2 and continues cutting behind #2 and #1.

(d) The drill continues until all five men reach the other end of the floor where they halt and wait until it becomes their turn to return down the floor using the same procedure.

(e) The drill should be performed slowly and the players encouraged to cut sharply so that a maximum number of passes can be made before reaching the opposite end of the floor.

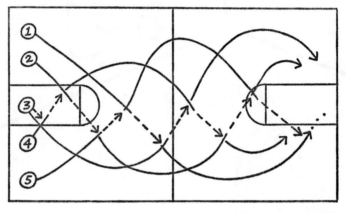

Diagram 28

29. *Learning to Meet the Pass*

The primary objective of this drill is to develop the habit among the players of meeting all passes.

Procedure:

(a) Divide the squad into two files facing each other about ten feet apart.

(b) Give the ball to the first man in one of the files. The first man passes to the opposite line's leader, who should break to meet the pass.

(c) The receiver, without dribbling, passes to the breaking man from the first file.

(d) The drill continues in this fashion.

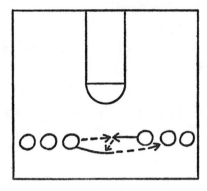

Diagram 29

30. Pivot Receiving Drill

This is not technically a passing drill at all, since all the emphasis should be placed on good receiving. Some big pivot men have trouble catching the ball. This drill will improve the catching ability of such players.

Procedure:

(a) Tape a piece of sponge rubber two inches wide and half an inch thick to the heel of each pivot man's hands.

(b) Place the guards in normal positions and have them pass to each pivot man as he moves out to take the pass at the free throw line. The pivot will receive from one guard and pass out to the other guard. The next pivot will receive from the guard who received the preceding pass.

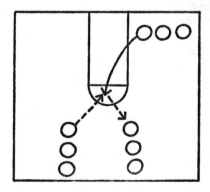

Diagram 30

31. Fingertip Passing Drill

The purpose of this drill is to get each player in the habit of passing and receiving with the fingers rather than with the palms of the hands.

Procedure:

(a) Have each player place his palms in loose chalk so that the chalk marks his palms but not his fingers.

(b) Have the men pass back and forth to each other in pairs, using all types of passes.

(c) After five minutes, inspect the ball used by each pair of players. Chalk marks will indicate that one of the men has been catching with the palms of his hands. Separate them and allow them to pass with two boys who have showed no chalk marks on their ball. In this way you can determine which boy is guilty of the fault.

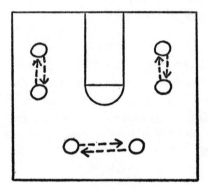

Diagram 31

6

Dribbling Drills

Dribbling is a vital basketball skill. Some coaches put little emphasis on dribbling because they have seen so many players use this fundamental unwisely. Players must be mature or wise enough to recognize the difference between a passing situation and a dribbling situation. If he lacks this wisdom, basketball will not be his best sport.

As a general statement, we can say that a dribble is wisely used when the dribbler is able to move around an opponent, get nearer to the goal, or set up a teammate for a shot. The skilled dribbler can pass off quickly and accurately when double teamed. He can change directions, switch hands and keep the ball on the outside, or the greatest possible distance from his defensive man. He can feint with head, eyes, hand, or shoulder. He possesses a change-of-pace motion and can start and stop suddenly. Last and possibly the most important facet of good dribbling is the ability to keep one's head up with clear vision to spot potential receivers.

The good dribbler is made—not born. The drills shown on the following pages should hasten this process.

1. Dribbling Through Line of Chairs

This is a popular drill that brings into focus sharp cutting, changing hands, and control of speed.

Procedure:

(a) Set up a row of six chairs from one base line to the other. Put the chairs about ten feet apart.

(b) Line the squad up facing the chairs. Give the first man a ball.

(c) The dribbler will start out by moving around the first chair to his right and then to his left around the second chair.

(d) The dribbler must change hands to keep the ball the maximum distance from each chair as he goes around it.

(e) The second player may begin after the first man has cleared the third chair.

(f) When all the men have gone through once, the same procedure may be used for the return trip.

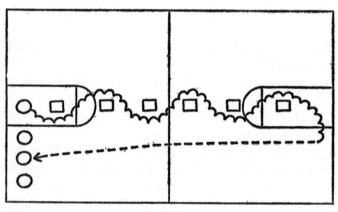

Diagram 1

2. Dribble Relay

Any time the spice of competition is added to practice, new spirit can be observed. In addition, this drill will point up the glaring error of trying to dribble faster than control will permit.

Procedure:

(a) Divide the squad into four groups. Station a group at the ends of each free throw line facing the center court.

(b) Each line should have the same number of boys.

(c) Give a ball to the first player in each line on one end of the floor.

(d) On the signal "go," these first men dribble as fast as control will allow to the man opposite his line on the other end of the floor. As he goes by, he bounce-passes to that man, who dribbles back to the second man in the first line.

(e) The drill can be ended when the last man has dribbled or when the first two men return to their original position.

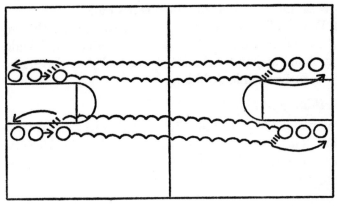

Diagram 2

3. *Switching Hands Dribble*

It is necessary that dribblers be able to switch hands without loss of efficiency. Here is a drill to help develop this ability.

Procedure:

(a) A line of players is formed at one end of the gymnasium.

(b) The first man will start out dribbling low, assuming that defensive men are approaching him.

(c) He dribbles diagonally across the floor until in danger of

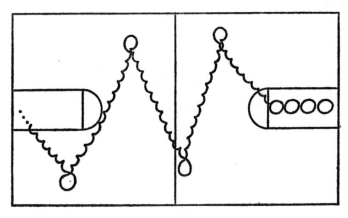

Diagram 3

getting too close to the sideline. Here he reverse pivots, keeping his eyes on the ball and continuing dribbling with the other hand.

(d) As soon as he clears the center line, which will take about two reverse pivots, the second man starts out.

(e) When all team members have completed this routine, have them return the length of the floor. Variety can be added by placing chairs at points where it is desired that players perform the reverse pivot while dribbling.

4. *Dribble and Handoff*

Many players have trouble giving a good handoff at the end of a dribble. This is especially true of the low dribble. Here is a very old formation and a drill that allows the coach an opportunity for close supervision and correction of errors.

Procedure:

(a) Form the squad into two groups with each group facing the other and standing side by side. Groups are about ten feet apart.

(b) The ball is given to the first man in one group and he dribbles in a low position to the first man in the other line. The dribbler picks the ball up at the end of the dribble to give a handoff.

(c) The first dribbler in the opposite line performs the same routine and hands off to the second man in the first group.

(d) The drill continues in this zig-zag fashion until all have performed.

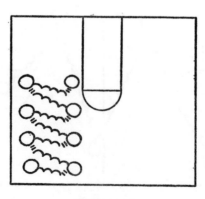

Diagram 4

(e) When the ball reaches the other end of the lines, the procedure is reversed and the drill starts again.

5. *Evading the Defensive Man*

Boys will often try to dribble past a defensive player who is in fairly good position. Yet we rarely practice this maneuver. We prefer players to pass rather than "fight" the defensive boy. However, there will be times when the dribbler is caught without a receiver and must be able to elude the defensive man.

Procedure:

(a) Using tape, mark a lane eight feet wide anywhere on the floor.

(b) Put one defensive boy in the lane with other members of his line standing well out of the drill area.

(c) An offensive line faces the lane with the first man holding a ball.

(d) The dribbler moves out and tries to avoid stepping out of the lane that has been marked and still dribble past the defensive player standing in the lane.

(e) After performing, all players exchange lines.

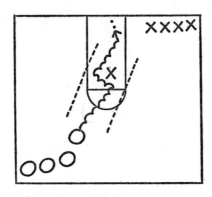

Diagram 5

6. *Signal Dribble Drill*

Here is another dribble drill that encourages the player to keep his head up. It also improves ability to start and stop quickly or to change direction.

Procedure:

(a) Give every player a ball and spread the squad out over one-half of the playing floor.

(b) The coach gets on the opposite free throw line to give hand signals.

(c) Signals are given with the hands and indicate directions. Forward, backward, left and right are the simplest. The coach may devise a signal for diagonal dribbling if he desires.

(d) Insist that the players keep heads up watching for the signals. One who misses a signal might put the ball down and run a certain number of laps if coaching policy has conditioned players to this sort of approach so that it will not have a negative value.

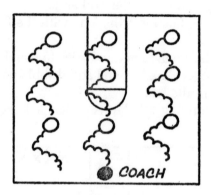

Diagram 6

7. Dribble Tag

This is a drill that players always receive with enthusiasm—a "fun" drill. It should help instill pep and life in the practice session.

Procedure:

(a) Place the entire squad on one half court.

(b) Designate a player to be "it."

(c) "It" dribbles continuously while making an effort to catch one of the other players

(d) All the other members of the squad try to avoid being touched by "it." When touched, a player becomes the dribbler.

(e) To impress all team members with the importance of staying out of the three second area, insist that they try to jump the lane when crossing it. Obviously, the dribbler cannot do this.

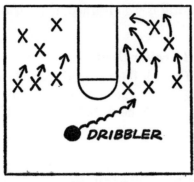

Diagram 7

8. *Four Corner Dribbling Drill*

The objective of this drill is to give a maximum number of players practice at the same time. This is also good as a method of developing the weak dribbling hand.

Procedure:

(a) Place a line in each corner of a half court.

(b) The player in line 1 dribbles to the first player in line 2. A shovel pass is given this player, who immediately hands the ball back to the first player. Both men move in the direction of line 3 with the first man still dribbling. At a half-way point between lines 2 and 3, the player from line 1 hands the ball to the

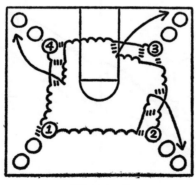

Diagram 8

first man from line 2, who dribbles to the first man in line 3. The same procedure continues until the ball goes around to all the lines. Players move from one line to the next after they have performed. After the drill is well learned, more balls can be put into action.

9. Dribbler and Trailer Drill

The objective of this drill is to teach each player to "see" everyone as he dribbles. Often the best move is to give the ball to a teammate who is behind the dribbler. The dribbler can then act as a screen for the trailer.

Procedure:

(a) Divide the team into two groups. Station one group in a corner of the floor and the other group diagonally across from them.

In this formation both groups can work at the same time.

(b) The first man in each group starts dribbling with a trailer moving behind him. After the dribbler has gone several steps he should stop quickly, side pass to the trailer, who will pick up the dribble and continue with the first man acting as a trailer. The drill continues in this manner until the players reach the opposite corner of the gymnasium.

(c) If a line starts out dribbling with the right hand, the line should make the return trip using the left hand.

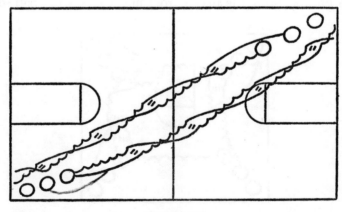

Diagram 9

10. *Two Ball Dribble Drill*

A pass is brought into play while performing this dribble drill. However, the main emphasis has to be put on one fundamental at a time and the dribble is most important in this drill.

Procedure:

(a) Divide the squad into four groups and place them in lines, forming a square around the center circle and about ten feet from the circle.

(b) A ball is given to the first man in lines 1 and 3.

(c) These men dribble to the edge of the center circle, face diagonally to their right and pass to the first man in that line.

(d) The first men in lines 2 and 4 receive these passes and perform the same ritual.

(e) After each performance the player will take the last position in the line on his right.

(f) The drill can be reversed by dribbling and passing to the line on the left.

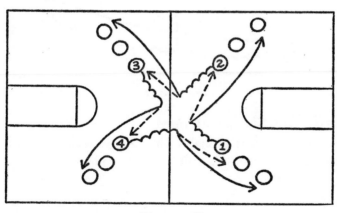

Diagram 10

11. *Chase the Dribbler*

Some boys become unnerved when a defensive man approaches them from the rear. The objective of this drill is to prepare for situations of this nature.

Procedure:

(a) Two lines are arranged in opposite corners of the gymnasium, with the first line in each corner two strides ahead of the second line.

(b) On a signal from the coach, the first men in all lines start toward the other basket.

(c) The first men in the front lines are the dribblers. The first men in the second line are the chasers.

(d) The chasers do everything possible to cause the dribblers to lose confidence and to prevent them from going on in for a lay-up.

(e) The dribbler and chaser change lines after they have performed.

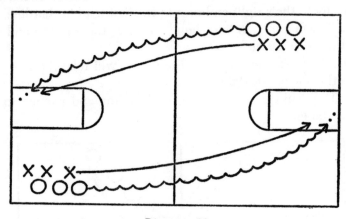

Diagram 11

12. *Dribbling Change of Pace*

A change of pace is probably the biggest weapon a dribbler can employ. The aim of this drill is to help youngsters acquire this basketball weapon.

Procedure:

(a) Station a manager on the free throw line.

(b) Line up all team members behind the center line facing the basket and the manager.

(c) The manager is instructed to jump at the dribbler as he performs his change of pace. When the manager jumps, the dribbler speeds up and goes on in for the basket.

(d) After the drill is well learned, instruct the manager to jump only on occasions when change of pace is performed properly. When the manager doesn't jump forward the dribbler should stop for a jump shot.

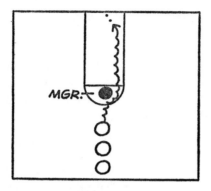

Diagram 12

13. *Loose Ball Recovery and Dribble*

The objective of this drill is to give players practice in picking up a free ball quickly, regaining balance, and cashing in on possession of the ball by going for a lay-up.

Procedure:

(a) Arrange the squad in four lines, forming a semi-circle that faces the coach, who stands under the goal.

(b) The coach rolls the ball toward the free throw line and the players take turns breaking for it, gaining possession and dribbling for the goal.

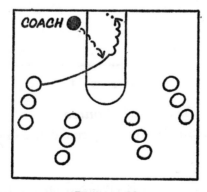

Diagram 13

14. Backward Dribble Drill

Sometimes the dribbler will get caught in a corner with no receivers in sight. His only alternative is to back out dribbling. Here is a drill to practice this maneuver.

Procedure:

(a) Two drills can be run simultaneously, one in each corner of a half court.

(b) Two lines are formed. The inside line is defensive and the outside line is the dribbling line.

(c) The dribbler starts to the corner closely guarded by the defensive man, who tries to get at the ball all the time the dribbler is performing. When the dribbler gets as far in the corner as possible, he will back out—still dribbling and protecting the ball from the defensive man.

(d) When the dribbler gets about half way back to the starting point he stops, turns away from the defensive man, and passes to the second man in his line.

(e) The performers exchange lines each time. The entire drill should be worked on both sides of the floor so that practice on each hand will occur.

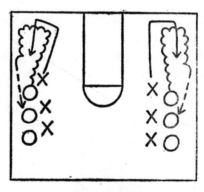

Diagram 14

15. Dribbling the Obstacle Course

The aim of this drill is to develop confidence in the dribbler.

Procedure:

(a) An obstacle course is arranged on the floor as shown in Diagram 15.

(b) Each player dribbles through the course, attempting to overcome each obstacle as it presents itself.

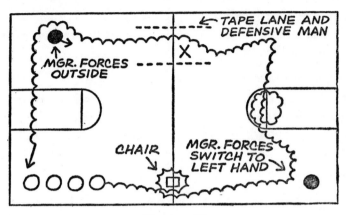

Diagram 15

16. Competitive Dribbling

Competitive dribbling is a drill that will give players practice in cutting sharply while moving at a high rate of speed.

Procedure:

(a) Divide the squad into two lines about ten feet apart and face them in the same direction.

(b) The last man in one line and the first man in the other line are given balls.

(c) On a signal from the coach, both boys move out, one drib-

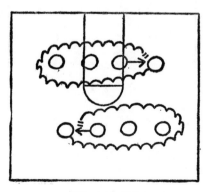

Diagram 16

bling with the left hand and one with the right hand. They will dribble around their own line completely and give the ball to the next man in line. Each dribbler tries to overtake the man who is dribbling against him.

(d) Vary the drill so that each line gets to practice with both the right *and* the left hand.

17. *Double Circle Dribble Drill*

The purpose of this drill is to teach players how to dribble in close quarters. It should also help prepare them for the last minutes of a game when the opponents are pressing and double teaming.

Procedure:

(a) Place ten men in one circle, with one defensive man in its exact center.

(b) Place three dribblers in the circle between middle man and the outside ring.

(c) All three dribblers dribble continuously, with the middle man staying in place and slapping at the basketballs. The men in the outside circle also stay in place but attempt to slap the ball away from the dribblers if they come too close to the circle.

(d) Change dribblers frequently.

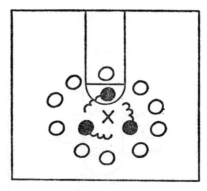

Diagram 17

18. *Circle Dribble Drill*

This drill will teach the players the importance of protecting the ball while it is being dribbled.

Procedure:

(a) Two lines of men are arranged facing each other on either side of a circle.

(b) The first man in each line gets in the circle and one is given a ball.

(c) On the coach's signal, the man with the ball begins to dribble low, staying in the circle at all times. He must protect the ball from the other man, who is trying to take it away from him.

(d) After one minute has elapsed, the coach will call time and two other men get in the circle.

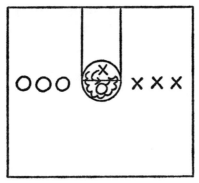

Diagram 18

19. Head up Dribbling Drill

This is a drill that will teach the players to keep heads up or receive a severe reminder.

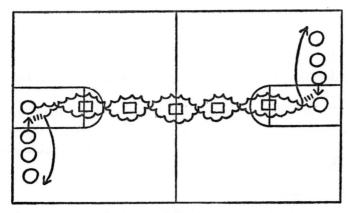

Diagram 19

Procedure:

(a) Place five chairs in a row, ten feet apart. Put a line of players at each end of the row of chairs.

(b) On the coach's signal, the first man in each line starts dribbling in a zig-zag manner through the chairs. If he does not keep his head up, he may collide with the dribbler coming from the other direction. These two go to the end of the opposite lines and two more start out at the same time as they finish.

20. *Practicing the Dribble with the Use of Vision Deterrents*

Blindfolds or dribble glasses may be used for this drill. The object is to train players to dribble without looking at the ball.

Procedure:

(a) Give each player a ball and a pair of dribble glasses or a blindfold.

(b) Station managers around the floor to warn the players who are working too close to each other.

(c) Start the boys off dribbling with the strongest hand and switch to the weak hand as soon as they develop some control.

21. *Fingertip Dribbling*

The objective of this drill is to develop fingertip control. It is necessary to relax and not fight the ball if this drill is to be successful.

Procedure:

(a) Give each player a ball and spread the squad over the entire floor.

(b) Each player spreads his legs wide and leans over so that he can dribble the ball in low six-inch bounces in and out between his legs.

(c) He dribbles the ball through his legs from the front and reaches behind to continue dribbling with the opposite hand.

(d) A good variation is to have the players use dribble glasses or blindfolds.

22. *Left-Handed Basketball*

Practically all young basketball players play almost entirely with the strong hand. Left alone or unsupervised they will not correct this, which points to the fact that most formal drills on lay-up shots, passing, and dribbling should be designed to improve the weak hand.

Procedure:

(a) Divide the team into groups of threes. Place six men, composing two of the groups, on one end of the floor and six men on the other end.

(b) A left or weak-handed game is played, especially using left-handed dribbling.

(c) The game should end at ten points. Another group that is waiting should be allowed to play the winners.

23. *Dribbling Wind Sprints*

Many teams end practice with wind sprints. To reach two objectives with one drill, give each player a ball and conduct the drill exactly the same except that all players are dribbling as they run.

7

Pivoting Drills

The center is usually associated with pivoting. At one time pivot drills were an integral part of every basketball practice session. During recent years, most of us have gradually acquired the idea that pivoting skill will be developed in free play. At any rate, little work is done that is aimed primarily at developing skill in this area.

The pivot is or should be a tool of every player, both offensively and defensively. In addition to teaching players to become adept at pivoting, drills in this category will develop body balance, split vision, and change of pace.

1. 180-Degree Turn Pivoting

Pivots are made that constitute all degrees of the possible 360-degree turn. Therefore, practice on all of these turns is needed. Here is a drill for the half turn.

Procedure:

(a) The team is placed in three lines. The first man in each line should have a ball.

(b) The first player in each line dribbles out about twelve feet, pivots 180 degrees with a rear pivot, and passes to the second man in line. The three lines perform simultaneously.

(c) All members of the lines perform in the same manner. After rear right and left pivots are practiced, front pivots should be given attention.

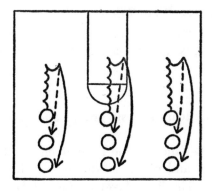

Diagram 1

2. Four Corner Practice of the 270-Degree Turn

The objective here is to practice on the three-quarter pivot, which is a little more difficult than the half turn.

Procedure:

(a) Align the squad in four lines twenty feet apart with all lines facing a player stationed in the center of the square thus formed. (See Diagram 2.)

(b) Two balls are used. The first players in lines 1 and 3 dribble to the center man, pivot and pass to the first men in lines 2 and 4.

(c) The drill continues in this fashion until all men in the formation have practiced pivoting and passing to the right and to the left.

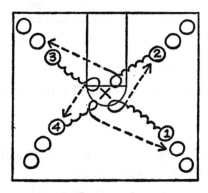

Diagram 2

3. *The 90-Degree Pivot Turn*

A pivot that is probably used more often than any other is the 90-degree turn. It is the easiest but should not be left out of the practice period.

Procedure:

(a) Divide the team into six groups and place them as shown in Diagram 3.

(b) The first two men in line 1 are given a ball. The first player dribbles to line 2 and pivots 90 degrees to the left to give that player a handoff. The first player in line 2 takes the handoff and performs the same movement with line 3. The drill continues as shown until line 6 is reached.

(c) When the first handoff is made, another ball can be put into action.

(d) The players exchange lines after every performance. Start the drill from the other end of the formation to vary the direction of the pivot.

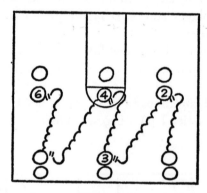

Diagram 3

4. *Three Corner Pivot Drill*

This is a drill to teach meeting the pass, quick stopping and pivoting.

Procedure:

(a) Arrange the squad in three lines. The lines should have considerable distance between them.

(b) The player in line 1 starts the drill by passing to the first man in line 2 who comes to meet the pass, stops immediately without dribbling, pivots right rear, and passes to the first man in line 3. This player executes the same movements as the player in line 2.

(c) The drill continues around the triangle. It can be varied to practice several degrees of turns by varying the line designated to be the first receiving line.

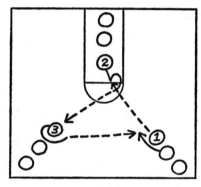

Diagram 4

5. *Cutting out the Defensive Man with a Pivot*

One of the best uses of the pivot is to evade a defensive man. Here is a drill to practice this maneuver.

Procedure:

(a) Form two lines just inside the center line on one half court.

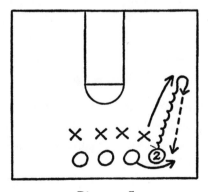

Diagram 5

(b) The inside line is composed of defensive men and the outside line of offensive players.

(c) The first man in line 2 dribbles to a point where he is in danger of being forced too close to the side line, stops, pivots 45 degrees, and passes underhanded with the left hand to the second man in line 2.

(d) The performers then exchange lines. The drill should be run on each side of the floor to develop ambidexterity.

6. Full Turn Pivot Practice

It is rare that a player is forced to turn a full 360 degrees. It is performed best by using two half-turns. Here is a drill to prepare for the possibility of such an emergency.

Procedure:

(a) Two lines are formed facing each other some ten feet apart.

(b) The first player in line 1 dribbles to the halfway point, stops, pivots half way around with a rear pivot facing the opposite line, and passes to the first player in that line.

(c) The drill continues in this manner until all players have participated.

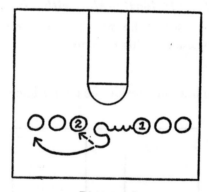

Diagram 6

7. Mass Formation Squad Pivot Practice

A simple formation to give every boy much practice in using the easier pivots is offered here. It can be performed with or without the possession of a ball.

Procedure:

(a) Place the squad in any formation that will allow the coach maximum opportunity for observation from where he stands.

(b) On a command from the coach, the entire squad pivots in a manner indicated by the name of the command.

(c) The commands that may be used are: right rear, left rear, left front, right front, half right front, and so on.

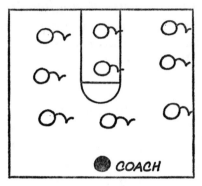

Diagram 7

8. Rear Pivot and Handoff

Often the termination of a dribble necessitates a pivot. This is a method of giving large numbers of players a great deal of practice in a relatively short time.

Procedure:

(a) Any number of lines can work this drill. It is best to have enough so that only two men are in each line.

(b) The first man in each line is standing one step in front of the man behind him.

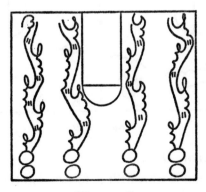

Diagram 8

(c) The first man pivots. The second man moves quickly, takes a handoff and comes to a jump stop. This jump stop carries him about a step ahead of the first man, who comes by for the handoff and a jump stop halt without putting the ball on the floor for a dribble.

9. *Cutting out the Defensive Man When Pressed*

The pivot is of invaluable aid in beating a press. Here is a drill that might well be an actual method of advancing the ball past center line when the defensive team is pressing.

Procedure:

(a) Divide the squad into four groups and station them as shown in Diagram 9.

(b) The dribbler can "point" the defensive man inside or outside to set him up for the cut-out pivot.

(c) The trailer must cut by for a handoff according to whether the pivot man is cutting the defensive man inside or outside.

(d) At a point just this side of the center line, the dribbler stops and using a rear pivot, cuts the defensive man out, and hands off to the trailer who is cutting fast.

(e) The performers swap lines and also practice on the opposite side of the floor before the drill is discontinued.

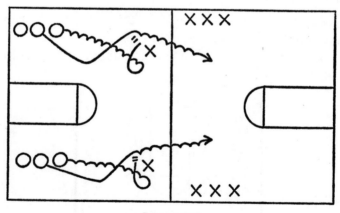

Diagram 9

10. *Circle Pivot Drill*

The primary aim of this drill is to develop the ability to pivot quickly and stay on balance.

Procedure:

(a) Place five players in a circle with a radius of twelve feet. Any number of circles can be used.

(b) The ball is given to any player who pivots, passes to the next man in the circle. The receiver pivots and passes to the next man.

(c) The drill continues around the circle, using any number of different types of pivots.

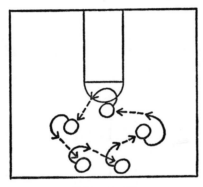

Diagram 10

11. *Reverse Pivot Drill*

This is a drill that is useful for every player. Normally the forwards and the pivot will find the most use for this action.

Procedure:

(a) Set up a triangular formation as shown in Diagram 11.

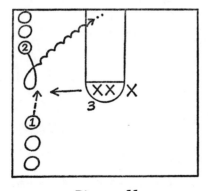

Diagram 11

(b) The passer in line 1 throws the ball to the player from line 2. Before the pass is made, the first man from line 3 steps into defensive position directly behind the first man from line 2. As the ball hits his hands the receiver reverse pivots in either direction and drives for the basket.

(c) Rotation from line to line is in clockwise fashion.

12. Pivot and Recovery Drill

This drill is designed to teach players how to pivot and get the ball in the range of vision quickly.

Procedure:

(a) Three men are placed in any number of lines about ten feet from a gymnasium wall.

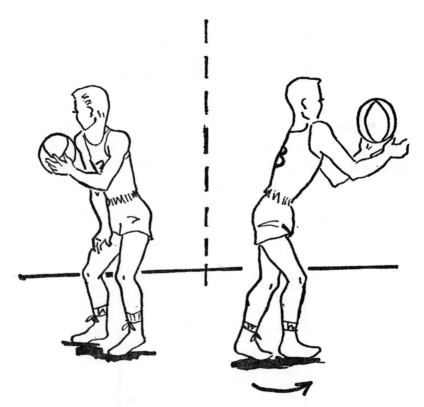

Sketch for Drill #12. Pivot and Recovery Drill.

(b) With backs to the wall, the performers will look over their right shoulders and pass the ball so that it hits the wall hard about three feet above the floor.

(c) The performers then pivot quickly in the direction away from the ball, visually locate the ball and receive their own pass.

(d) Each man should take five tries before moving to the end of the line.

(e) The pass should be made with one hand and then the other to insure a variety of rebounds and recoveries.

8

Rebounding Drills

Rebounding is the work horse of basketball. It is the drab, thankless task performed by steady performers. It is the "blood and guts" of the game.

All players appreciate a good rebounder. They appreciate good rebounding most when it is being done by someone else. A lot of good shooters fail to appreciate the value of rebounds but will break their necks to try for a tip-in. Such players have not been properly conditioned mentally. Most teams reserve the greatest respect and admiration for their high rebounders and this is as it should be.

Basketball is being played by bigger and bigger boys. There are few weak players. It takes real courage to get under the goal with all the flying elbows and knees. There is no protective padding in this game, either. The only way youngsters will develop rebound courage and skill is by drilling. Players do not miraculously become rebounders by use of half-time talks. The practice session is the time to separate the "horses from the mules." Here are some drills that should help the coach to accomplish this objective. Many of the rebounding and the tipping drills are interchangeable.

1. Competitive Rebounding

The purpose of this drill is to provide a game-type situation so that players will get some opposition as they go up on the board.

Procedure:

(a) Arrange the squad in three lines forming a semi-circle and facing a basket.

(b) The first man in line 1 takes a short shot and goes for the rebound. At the same time the first men from lines 2 and 3 go for the rebound.

(c) The second men in all the lines perform in the same manner.

(d) After every one has participated, have a different line do the shooting.

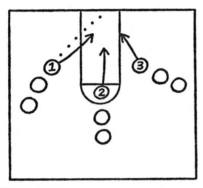

Diagram 1

2. *Defensive Rebounding*

The purpose of this drill is to teach players to block opponents away from the goal on defensive rebounds.

Diagram 2

Procedure:

(a) Arrange the men in three lines facing a basket.

(b) The first men in each line step out two strides and face away from the goal.

(c) The coach throws the ball up on the board and the second men race for the rebound. The first men pivot, block them off and take the rebound.

(d) The defensive rebounders go to the end of the line and the offensive rebounders take their places.

3. Race for Rebound Position

The aim here is to give men practice in moving long distances to get into rebound position. They should learn not to come roaring in for a broad jump rebound, which usually causes them to foul someone.

Procedure:

(a) The team is divided into two groups and placed in lines at what are the forward positions for most teams.

(b) The first men in each line step forward, turn their backs to the goal and become defensive rebounders. The second men will be offensive rebounders.

(c) The coach tosses a ball up on the boards from about the head of the circle. All four participants race for the ball. The defensive players should block the offensive men's paths.

(d) The performers then exchange positions in the lines so that all will get to participate in each position.

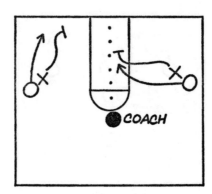

Diagram 3

4. *Grasping the Ball Firmly*

This drill is designed to teach players to "clutch" when the hands make contact with the ball. Otherwise, some players will tip it out, or take it with one hand. Some are often shaken loose from the ball also.

Procedure:

(a) Attach an iron bar to a wall at a height of about twelve feet. Let the bar project from the wall at least two feet.

Sketch for Drill #4. Grasping the Ball Firmly.

(b) Attach a strong car tire inner tube to the bar and to a ball so that the ball dangles from the bar at a height of ten feet. Cradle the ball in the loop of the inner tube; then tie a strong cord around the tube just above the ball to secure the ball.

(c) Have the players take turns jumping, taking the ball and pulling it down until their feet strike the floor.

5. Practicing the Jackknife Rebound

The objective of this drill is to teach players to twist off the boards to one side with a jackknife after clutching the ball firmly.

Procedure:

(a) Place a line of players at a basket, with a manager to toss the ball up against the boards.

(b) Place another line directly in front of the goal with the first man too far under the goal.

(c) The ball is tossed on one side of the basket, directly in front of the line facing that side of the board. The first man in that line jumps, grasps the ball, and jacknifes away from the player in the other line.

(d) Players exchange lines.

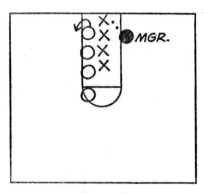

Diagram 5

6. Free-Throw Position Drill

The purpose of this drill is to develop the habit of jockeying for that good rebound position after a free throw is made.

Procedure:

(a) Station two lines on either side of the basket as shown on the diagram.

(b) The coach stands on the free throw line and calls any signal he desires to start the drill. A good signal is a long, drawn out preparatory command of "r-e-a-d-y-e-e--" and a short, sharp "HUP!" as the command for action.

(c) Each inside man will then step across the lane quickly with his outside foot. The outside men try to prevent them from getting this position.

(d) The men will then exchange lines.

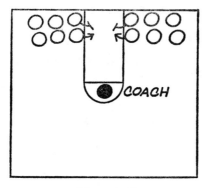

Diagram 6

7. *One on One Drill*

The spirit of competition is added to rebounding here, and an actual game-type situation is created.

Procedure:

(a) Place the squad in two lines facing the goal. The first

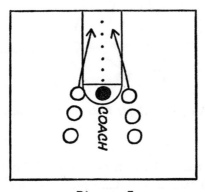

Diagram 7

men in each line will be standing about a yard in front of the free throw line and outside of the lane.

(b) The coach stands between them and tosses the ball so that it rebounds straight off the front of the boards.

(c) Both of the first men in each line break for the rebound, fighting for position. They try to jacknife away when possession is gained.

(d) These players then go to the end of the line as the second men compete in the same fashion.

(e) Try to pair boys of equal jumping ability.

8. *Wall Drill Rebounding*

Here is a good drill to give the entire squad a jumping workout in a short period of time.

Sketch for Drill #8. Wall Drill Rebounding.

Procedure:

(a) Place the entire team in pairs spread out around the wall.

(b) Give each pair a ball. One player tosses the ball up and the other boy jumps, grasps, jacknifes, and comes down with the ball.

(c) The player who tossed the ball tries to tie the rebounder up for a held ball.

(d) If a held ball situation is achieved, the same man will jump again until he is successful in coming down and retaining full possession of the ball. If a held-ball situation does not occur, the other man will jump for the ball.

9

Tipping Drills

Tipping a basketball into the basket is a spectacular feat of timing, coordination, and jumping ability. Players rarely need encouragement to work on this phase of the game.

Some sports writers and coaches have referred to such goals as cheap baskets. Investigations would probably prove that the scorer has spent hours of jumping and tipping at a practice goal. Tipping is a skill we cannot afford to overlook. It gives the boy with leg spring an opportunity to double his scoring power. Several tip-ins in a game can mean the difference between victory and defeat.

Obviously, leg strength is a primary prerequisite. Position and timing are the most important aspects of tipping skill. However, without practice, all the physical qualifications will still cause a player to be impotent as a tipper.

"Sell" the players on the value of tipping. Practice tipping. Keep charts to show the results of practice efforts. Do not allow indiscriminate "slapping" at the ball. Here are some drills that will insure maximum dividends from the time spent on this facet of the game.

1. Toss and Tip Drill

Players will learn to adjust to direction of rebound while performing this drill.

110

Procedure:

(a) Place the squad in two lines facing a goal. Give the first man in each line a ball.

(b) The first man in the left line tosses the ball against the board and moves quickly out of the way as the second man uses his left hand to tip the ball in the goal.

(c) The first man in the right line tosses the ball against the board and moves quickly out of the way as the second man tips the ball in the goal, using his right hand.

(d) The drill continues in this manner until the end of the line is reached. Players should arrange themselves on a second round so that those who threw the ball up for the tippers will become tippers.

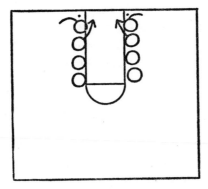

Diagram 1

2. *Triangular Tipping Formation*

The purpose of this drill is to practice closing out the defense so that the boy with the best position can tip easier.

Procedure:

(a) Situate the squad around the goal in three lines forming a semi-circle and facing the basket.

(b) The first three men are tippers. The second three men ride the backs of the first three. The coach tosses the ball against the board. The player with the best position tries to tip in the goal as the other two players block for him.

(c) The first men go to the end of the line and the second men become tippers. Alternate the lines.

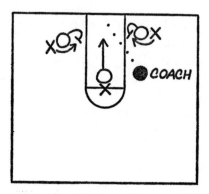

Diagram 2

3. Special Tipping Ring Practice

A small target necessitates a fine aim. In this drill the goal is made as small as possible, yet allowing the ball to go through it.

Procedure:

(a) Attach a small inner ring, sixteen inches in circumference, to the regular goal.

(b) Place a player on either side of the basket. Let one player start the drill by tossing the ball up on the boards. Both men attempt to tip the ball in the goal.

Sketch for Drill #3. Special Tipping Ring Practice.

4. Timing For the Tip

This drill will develop a sense of timing that comes from jumping exactly the right height for the tip.

Procedure:

(a) Place a cover securely over the regular basket so that the ball cannot go through the goal.

(b) Station three players around the goal. One player should toss the ball and all three tip it each time it comes off the edge of the covered rim.

(c) Let the players alternate positions.

Sketch for Drill #4. Timing for the Tip.

5. Tether Ball Tipping

Tether ball tipping allows the player to get the thrill of tipping the ball into the basket. It also allows a great deal of practice in only a few minutes.

Procedure:

(a) Give the manager a tether ball (with rope attached). Let him climb up or use a ladder to assume a position on top of the backboard.

(b) A player is stationed on either side of the basket.

(c) The manager holds the ball at rim height and twelve inches away from the rim. As the players tip the ball into the goal, the manager jerks it out and the players tip it whenever it becomes stationary.

(d) Players should work on both sides of the goal.

Sketch for Drill #5.   Tether Ball Tipping.

6.   Volleyball Basketball

The objective of this drill is to develop leg stamina and timing.

Procedure:

(a) A line of players is formed on either side of the goal, facing the basket.

(b) The first man in each line is given the ball. He tosses the ball against the board and taps it against the board five times, as though dribbling it on the floor. On the sixth jump, he uses both hands to tap it into the goal.

(c) The next player takes a turn. Each performer goes to the end of the opposite line after his turn.

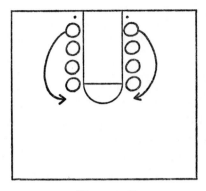

Diagram 6

7. Two on One

The aim of the following is to provide game-type competition.

Procedure:

(a) Three lines are formed, one on either side of the goal and one facing the goal.

(b) The middle line is defensive.

(c) The ball is thrown against the goal and the first men from the two outside lines try to tip it in the basket. The middle man tries to stop them.

(d) The players will alternate lines.

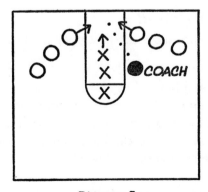

Diagram 7

8. *Alternate Tipping*

Here is a conditioning drill that also helps to develop timing.

Procedure:

(a) Place a line on either side of the goal and facing it.

(b) The first two men start the drill. One tosses the ball against the board behind the basket so that it caroms off on the opposite side, in front of the other man. The player on that side immediately tips it all the way across the board to the other man by banking it off the board. This continues until each man has made ten jumps without a miscue.

(c) The next two men take a turn, and so on until all players have participated. After participation, each player takes his place at the end of the opposite line.

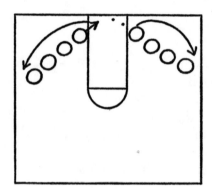

Diagram 8

9. *Dot on the Wall Drill*

Improving the accuracy of the tipper is the aim here.

Procedure:

(a) Paint several black dots on the wall at a height of ten feet. These can be painted with tempera paint, which will wash off.

(b) Station a line of players in front of each dot.

(c) The first man tosses the ball up against the wall and will tip rebound against the dot until he has struck the target five consecutive times.

(d) The next player takes a turn and so on down the line.

Sketch for Drill #9.   Dot on the Wall Drill.

10. Endurance Drill

The purpose of this drill is to evaluate the leg endurance of players and at the same time give them practice in jumping and tipping.

Procedure:

(a) Place a line of players in front of the basket.

(b) The first man tosses the ball against the boards and starts tipping. The other players count to determine how many times he can tip consecutively without an error.

(c) Every player takes a turn. Some record should be kept to determine the season champ.

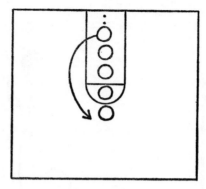

Diagram 10

11.   *Free Throw Tip-in Drill*

The objective here is to give practice in tipping, especially in a free throw situation.

Procedure:

(a) Place two men on each side of the free throw lane.

(b) Place one man on the free throw line as a shooter.

(c) After the shooter attempts the free throw, all three men try to tip the ball into the basket. If the shooter makes a goal, he shoots until he misses. If he misses, the player who is successful at tipping the rebound in the goal becomes the shooter.

(d) The players rotate in clockwise fashion unless one is successful at tipping the ball into the basket.

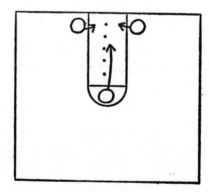

Diagram 11

10

Combination Drills

It seems inappropriate to place some drills in a specific fundamental category. Technically, every drill offers the opportunity
to improve in more than one way. For instructional purposes, to
improve team and individual weaknesses, the greater emphasis
should be placed on one skill at a time. This is especially sound
when dealing with *young* athletes.

A great number of basketball drills have evolved, however,
which aim for improvement of more than one skill. Such drills
are best suited for advanced performers. Stress can be placed on
any part of the drill. Coaches will sometimes vary the point of
emphasis with different players. The following drills are offered
as "combination drills." The reader may evaluate, select, and use
them while keeping his own particular offense in mind.

1. *Line Drill*

For practice of the dribble with the right and left hands, and
for practice of the hook pass and receipt of a handoff prior to
starting a fast dribble.

Procedure:

(a) Place five men in a straight line.

(b) The first man in line dribbles to a spot ten feet from the
second man. At this point he turns and gives the second man a
hook pass. #1 then breaks fast for a handoff from his receiver.

After taking the handoff, #1 dribbles fast with his left hand until he has circled the line.

(c) After dribbling around the line #1 hands the ball to #2, who performs in the same manner. #1 goes to the end of the line.

(d) This drill can be varied so that the dribbler will make his circle while dribbling with his right hand.

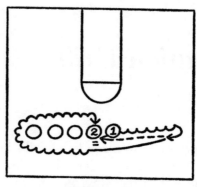

Diagram 1

2. Steal the Bacon Drill

Here is a drill that adds the element of competition. It requires aggressiveness and quick reactions.

Procedure:

(a) Line the entire squad up on one half court by placing half on one side line and half on the other.

(b) Have each line count off. One team will count off from the center line to the base line. The other team will count off from the base line to the center line. Each line will have an equal number of men and corresponding numbers.

(c) The coach rolls the ball to any point half way between the lines and calls a number. Those players on each side whose number is called break for the ball. The player who obtains possession will try to score. The other man tries to prevent him. If the attempt to score is successful, that team gets two points. If the defensive man thwarts the scoring attempt, his team gets two points.

(d) The coach should remember to call all numbers so that everyone gets to perform.

(e) After the drill is well learned, more than one number can be called in order to create situations of two on two, three on three, etc.

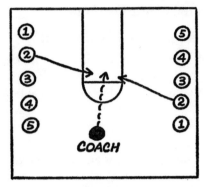

Diagram 2

3. Passing, Conditioning, and Footwork Drill

The slide step is all-important to the game of basketball. Many so-called skilled players do not execute this footwork properly without crossing the feet. Here is a drill to help correct this deficiency. Chest passing and stamina are other facets that should be improved through use of this drill.

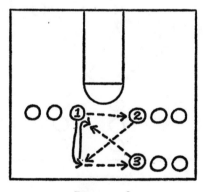

Diagram 3

Procedure:

(a) Arrange the squad in three lines with the first man in lines 1 and 3 ten feet from the first man in line 2.

(b) #1 passes to the first man in line 2 and slide steps about ten feet to his right. #2 feeds him a pass at this point and #1 passes to #3. He then slide steps back to position, where #3 will hit him with a return pass.

(c) All players rotate after performing.

4. Dribble Hook Pass and Lay-up Drill

The purpose of this drill is to simulate as closely as possible an actual game type situation. It will also give the players a remedy for solving this particular problem when they face it in competition.

Procedure:

(a) Station two offensive lines and one defensive line as shown in Diagram 4.

(b) Player #1 dribbles with his left hand toward the basket and defensive player #2 forces him toward the sideline. #3 breaks for the basket, receives a left-hand jump hook pass from #1, and goes for a left-hand lay-up.

(c) Alter the drill by running it in the same manner to the other side of the floor.

(d) Players should change lines after each performance.

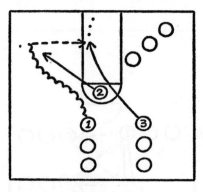

Diagram 4

5. Pivot and Lay-up Drill

After pivoting, some players have difficulty getting oriented with the basket. Here is a good drill to teach proper floor orientation at all times.

Procedure:

(a) Put one line of players out of bounds to feed the ball to another line of players stationed in bounds. These in-bounds players are to become the performers.

(b) The first player in line breaks for the basket. After two or three steps he stops, pivots, and continues. As soon as he comes out of his pivot, the player with the ball who is standing out of bounds feeds him a pass. The in-bounds player then goes in for a lay-up, using a dribble if it is necessary.

(c) This is a good time to practice down the base line lay-ups.

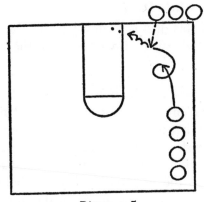

Diagram 5

6. Screening Drill

This drill could also be used as a warm-up. Its primary purpose is to teach players how to use a moving screen.

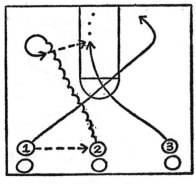

Diagram 6

Procedure:

(a) Arrange the squad in three lines on a half court.

(b) The first player in line 1 passes to the first man in line 2.
#1 cuts in front of #2, who uses a left-hand dribble in cutting
behind the moving screen set by 1. At a point to the left of the
basket, the dribbler stops, pivots and feeds the cutter from line
3, who also breaks off the moving screen set by #1. #3 goes for
the left-hand lay-up.

(c) Change the drill so that just the opposite actions are required by running it to the other side of the floor.

7. *Passing Foot Slide Drill*

The purpose of this drill is to develop the ability to slide step
to make progress sideward without crossing the legs.

Procedure:

(a) Place five men side by side and ten feet apart.

(b) Put a line of men ten feet from the first man in this line
of five and facing that man. The line of five are stationary.

(c) The first performer passes to the first man opposite him
and starts sliding sideward as he waits for the return pass. He
will continue down the line passing and receiving from each of
the five men. The return trip is made in the same manner. Each
man in the line takes his turn. The five stationary men are also
worked into the drill by rotating players.

(d) Any type of pass may be used that the coach feels the
team needs to develop.

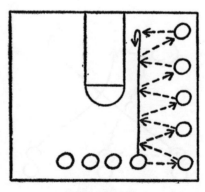

Diagram 7

8. Set Shooting Relay

This drill becomes a combination drill because it involves passing and dribbling. Its purpose is to teach the players to shoot cooly when an attempt is made to hurry them.

Procedure:

(a) Two lines are placed at one end of the floor. The first man in each line has a ball.

(b) On a signal from the coach, each player dribbles to the head of the circle on the other end of the floor. At this point, he attempts to score with a set or a jump shot. If he misses, he must retrieve the ball, hurry back and try until he does make the basket. After scoring he will make a baseball pass to the second man in his line, who must go through the same procedure.

(c) The line which finishes first is the winner.

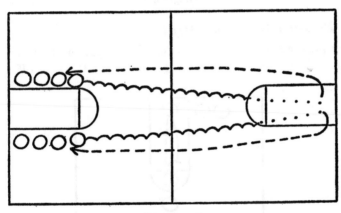

Diagram 8

9. Drill to Teach Stopping and Pivoting Under Control

This drill has a movement that is often employed by advanced players in the game of basketball. It is difficult to master and therefore is probably little worked on in formal practice.

Procedure:

(a) Place all the players in lines behind the forward slots.

(b) The first player in the right line is given a ball. The first player in the left line breaks to the free throw area, stops quickly as soon as the pass from the first man in the right line hits his hands, reverse pivots, and dribbles with the left hand for a lay-up.

(c) Players will exchange lines and the drill will be run from both sides of the floor.

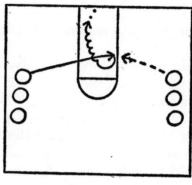

Diagram 9

10. *Pressure Jump Shot Drill*

The purpose of this drill is to teach the players to *take* plenty of time when they have plenty of time to get the shot off.

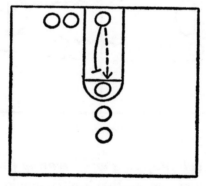

Diagram 10

Procedure:

(a) Divide the squad into two lines. Place one of them at the free throw line and the other behind the goal.

(b) The first man under the goal passes to the first man on the free throw line and rushes out to guard him as this receiver takes a jump shot.

(c) The shooter and the defensive man exchange lines as the next two men perform.

(d) This drill can be run from any angle or distance.

11

Fast Break Drills

All drills that involve passing, dribbling, or any of the skills discussed thus far would actually contribute to the development of a fast break attack. In view of the tremendous importance of fast breaking to the game of basketball, it seems necessary to add a section devoted entirely to fast break drills. The team is rare that doesn't fast break from at least one of the situations we consider opportune for the fast break. These situations are: after a rebound, free throw, jump ball, intercepted pass and field goal. Drills may be found in this chapter that cover all these situations except the jump ball. Drills for fast-breaking after a jump ball may be found in Chapter 18. Many teams who do not employ the fast break in games will use these drills to develop quicker reactions while on the move.

1. Long Pass Drill

The purpose of this drill is to develop long pass accuracy and receiving ability.

Procedure:

(a) Arrange the squad in four lines, one line at each corner of the floor.

(b) The first player in line 1 starts dribbling toward center court as the first player in line 2 breaks fast down the side line and cuts for the basket at the opposite end of the floor. The dribbler hits him with a long pass about half way between the head of the circle and center court. The receiver dribbles on in for the lay-up.

(c) As soon as these two players clear the floor, #3 and #4 perform the same drill moving toward the other end of the floor.

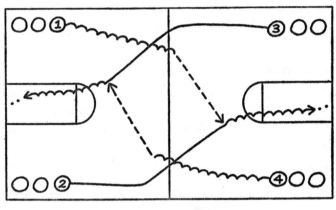

Diagram 1

2. Three Man Long Pass Drill

The three man long pass drill is designed to teach the players how to hit a stationary target with a long pass.

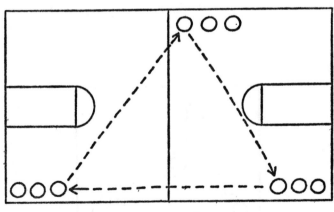

Diagram 2

Procedure:

(a) Place one line of men in the corner of the floor facing

another line on the same side of the floor, but in the corner at the other end. Place another line at center court on the opposite side line.

(b) The ball is passed from the corner to the center man to the other corner and back to the first man in a triangular fashion. Any type pass may be used but the baseball pass is probably the strongest one for this particular drill.

(c) Exchange the men frequently and be sure to work the drill from both sides of the floor.

3. *Two Man Half Court Break*

It is not always possible to have a three-lane attack on a fast break, even though it is to be desired. Here is a drill that gives practice to two men in situations where they will have a fast break advantage.

Procedure:

(a) Station the squad on either side line at center court in two lines.

(b) The first player in the left file dribbles once, hits the cutter from the right file at the head of the circle with a pass, and breaks for the basket for the return pass and a lay-up.

(c) These two players will exchange lines, and after every team member has performed the drill should be run to the other side of the floor.

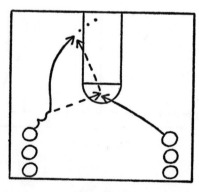

Diagram 3

4. Fast Break Drill Using the Dribble

The objective here is to teach the players to move the ball on down the floor quickly, looking for a play even though an open receiver is not immediately spotted.

Procedure:

(a) Place the squad in three lines. One line is composed of forwards placed in one corner of the floor. On the other end of the floor, in the corner, station the guards. All pivot men are placed under the basket on the same end with the forwards.

(b) The first guard dribbles to half court and makes a pass to the first forward, who breaks out to meet the pass. The forward turns and passes to the first pivot man who breaks to the free throw line and passes to the guard. This guard is cutting around the forward for the pass and a lay-up.

(c) All players return to the same line and the next three men perform. Run this drill to both sides of the floor.

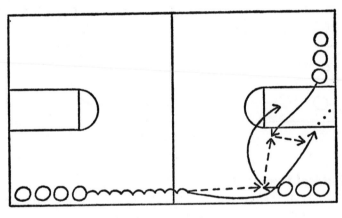

Diagram 4

5. Three Lane Fast Break Drill

This drill is designed to practice the three-on-one situation.

Procedure:

(a) Station three lines at one end of the gymnasium with the coach standing nearby. Place one man on the free throw line at the opposite end of the floor. The coach has the ball.

(b) The object of the drill is to take the ball down the middle of the floor. If the coach passes to the middle, that man will dribble to the free throw line at the other end of the gymnasium, where he will pass to one of the cutters in the outside line.

(c) If the coach passes to one of the outside lines, the receiver has a decision to make. He can dribble the ball to the center lane or he can pass it to the middle man.

(d) If the receiver dribbles to the center lane, the middle man moves to become a side cutter. If the side man passes to the middle lane, he continues in his regular lane.

(e) Members of the various lines should change places often so that all have an opportunity to become the middle man at one time or another.

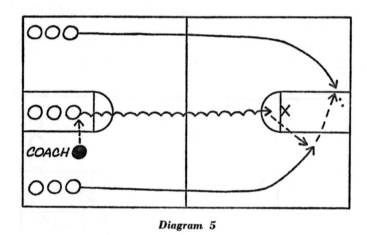

Diagram 5

6. Lateral Pass Drill

Here is a drill that will develop the ability to pass laterally to a receiver while the passer and receiver both are moving.

Procedure:

(a) Station all men in two files at one end of the floor.

(b) The first man in each file moves out simultaneously and these two men pass back and forth to each other all the way to the end of the floor.

(c) As soon as these players have cleared the half court, the second men in each file move out, passing back and forth without dribbling to the other end of the gymnasium.

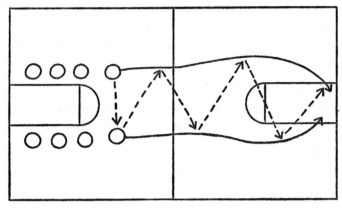

Diagram 6

7. Quick Pass After Rebound

Fast-breaking teams appear to get the ball moving down the court before the rebounder even comes down with the ball. Although this appears to be an illusion, it does actually happen. The value of this technique is questionable, and many teams feel that the risk of a poor pass on such a play is of doubtful value. However, a drill to help initiate such a fast start down the floor is offered here.

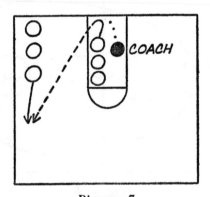

Diagram 7

Procedure:

(a) Divide the group into two lines and place them in the positions indicated by Diagram 7.

(b) The coach or manager may toss the ball up on the backboard. The first man in file 1 jumps and takes the ball in the air, attempting to twist off the boards for a pass to the first man in the outside file, who is breaking for the other basket.

(c) The receiver passes back to the coach and the participants exchange lines.

8. Circle Fast Break Drill

The aim of this drill is to teach the players to find their cutting lane quickly, no matter who should become the middle man.

Procedure:

(a) Divide the team into groups of five men. Put one group in a keyhole circle at one end of the floor. Place the ball in the center of the circle.

(b) On a signal from the coach all five players try to recover the ball. The player who obtains possession becomes the middle man. The other players become cutters, the trailer, or the safety, as predesignated by the coach.

(c) As soon as this group clears the other goal, another group of five move into the keyhole circle to perform the same drill.

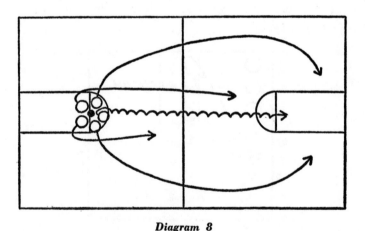

Diagram 8

9. Fast Break Drill from Defensive Positions

Here is a drill that helps impress the players with the importance of getting the ball off the backboard and down floor to the middle man quickly.

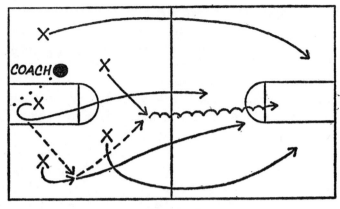

Diagram 9

Procedure:

(a) Divide the team into groups of five men. Place one group in defensive positions at one end of the floor.

(b) The coach or the manager will toss the ball against the backboard where the pivot or middle defensive man retrieves and passes to one of the corner defensive men. The receiver then passes to the guard on the opposite side of the floor, who breaks toward the middle for the pass and becomes the middle lane dribbler.

(c) The other guard becomes one of the side line cutters and the other forward becomes the other side line cutter.

(d) As soon as these men have cleared center line, another group will get into position quickly to run the same drill.

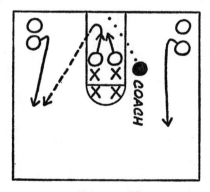

Diagram 10

10. Rebounding Fast Break Drill

This is a drill that develops the quick pass to the side line that is so necessary after a rebound if the fast break is to be successful.

Procedure:

(a) Arrange the squad in four lines underneath one goal.

(b) The two middle lines will have offensive players facing them.

(c) The two outside lines are the cutters. The ball is tossed on the backboard by the coach and the two middle men, who are in defensive positions, move for the rebound. They block out the offensive players and take the rebound, which is passed quickly to the cutter on the same side of the floor.

11. Fast Breaking After a Stolen Pass

This situation catches the defense off guard. It is a fine opportunity for a cheap basket which should be capitalized upon.

Procedure:

(a) Place three lines on one end of the floor.

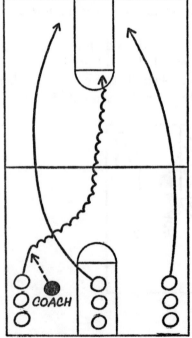

Diagram 11A   Diagram 11B

(b) The coach throws the ball to a player, who either passes to the middle man or dribbles to the middle. The other two players immediately break to become the side line cutters.

(c) A good variation is for the coach to toss the ball high or to roll it on the floor between two of the lines. The two players involved will have to adjust quickly after one of them gains possession.

12. Four Lane Attack

The objective of this drill is to develop quick positioning by the three front men and to employ the fourth man as a trailer.

Procedure:

(a) Divide the team into groups of four. Place one group on the floor at one end with the two outside men being guards and the two inside men being forwards or pivot men.

(b) The coach or a manager throws the ball against the backboard. The inside man who retreives the ball passes to the guard on his side. The guard breaks to a position near center line, about a yard from the side line. He is a stationary target.

(c) Upon receipt of the pass this guard passes to the other guard. The other guard breaks for the center of the floor to become the middle man.

(d) The first guard and the forward who has not so far been in action become the side line cutters. The forward who retrieved the rebound will become the trailer.

(e) To add some spice to this drill, place a defensive man on the free throw line of the goal to which the fast break is moving.

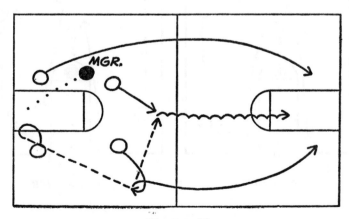

Diagram 12

13. *Fast Break Drill from a Missed Free Throw*

The purpose of this drill is to provide a method of fast breaking when the opponent can be caught unawares after a missed free throw.

Procedure:

(a) Divide the team into several groups of five men. Place three men under the basket in normal defensive position. Place the other two on either side, halfway between the side line and free throw lane.

(b) The missed free throw is tapped to one of the side line men. He dribbles and looks for the middle man coming from the free throw lane. That player who was originally stationed nearest the free throw line takes the middle lane. The guard who receives the tap and dribbles out will pass to this middle man. The middle man then moves down the floor with two side line cutters. These

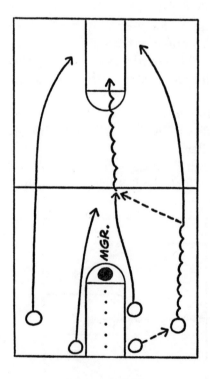

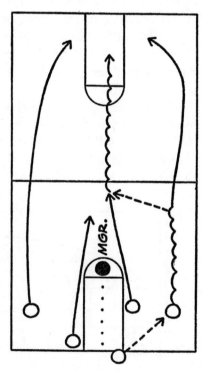

Diagram 13A   Diagram 13B

are the men who were originally placed between the side line and the free throw lane. The player under the goal, who has not thus far been employed, becomes the trailer.

(c) This drill can be worked from a free throw which is successful just as easily. Have the player who made the tap-out take the ball after the free throw, jump out of bounds, and pass the ball in bounds to one of the guards. From this point the drill will be performed just as if the goal were missed.

14. *Five Man Fast Break Drill*

This is a drill for breaking down floor after the rebound is secured.

Procedure:

(a) Arrange five men on one half court as shown in the diagram.

(b) Ordinarily the two outside men are guards. The middle man is the post man and the two side men are forwards.

(c) One of the outside men takes a shot. Both guards then break to the side lines. If a side man gets the rebound, he hits the guard on his side of the floor. If the middle man gets the rebound, he hits either guard on either side line.

(d) The side line receiver will hit the other guard breaking into the middle of the floor. This second guard will be the middle man on the fast break. The offside forward has come from under the basket to become the cutter on his side of the floor.

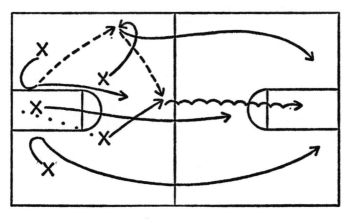

Diagram 14

(e) The deep man not involved in any way will become the trailer. The rebounder will become the safety man.

(f) As in all fast break drills employing the three lane attack, the two side cutters may go on under the basket and come out to position if they fail to receive or they may button hook back to position according to the particular follow up used by the various coaches.

12

Two and Three Man Scoring Drills

These drills should comprise at least a part of nearly every offense, especially those employing a single post. Drills of this nature can be adapted to all offenses. The coach will recognize those drills that will be of benefit to him in developing his system. The *set* and *pattern* continuity offenses will benefit most from this type of "part" breakdown practice. However, even the confirmed free lance coaches will see their boys make some of these plays through use of their own initiative. It seems most reasonable to believe that practicing them during the formal practice period would enable the coach to see them worked more often.

I. Two Man Drills

A. *Guard to Guard Scoring Drills*

If two men are to work a scoring play successfully, they must have space in which to operate. The forwards and pivot must open up the middle when these plays are worked. In practice, it is well to have all team members run them as drills. This gives the forwards and pivot a better understanding and appreciation of guard play. To work the entire team on these drills, line everyone up in two lines behind the guard spots. Two men will work together on each drill. When all the players have run it, and run it well, change the drill to the other side of the floor. All of these drills will work equally well on both sides of the floor. For purposes of clarification, the following abbreviations will be used:

LG . . . left guard
RG . . . right guard
LF . . . left forward
RF . . . right forward

1. Stationary Screen

Procedure:

(a) The LG passes to the RG and sets a screen for him.

(b) The RG foot fakes to his right and uses a low left-hand dribble to go all the way in for a left-hand lay-up.

(c) Work this drill from RG to LG after everyone has run it from left to right.

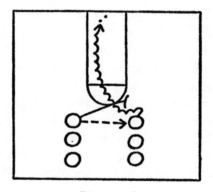

Diagram 1

2. Roll out

Procedure:

(a) The LG passes to the RG and sets a one count screen for him before rolling (by pivoting rearward on the left foot) for the basket, looking over his left shoulder.

(b) The RG foot fakes to the right while the screen is being set, recovers, and passes to the breaking LG at a point which allows him to go up immediately for a left-hand lay-up.

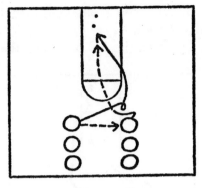

Diagram 2

3. Dribbling Screen

Procedure:

(a) The LG dribbles low with the right hand toward his RG's defensive man.

(b) When the LG gets two yards from the defensive man, the RG foot fakes to his right and cuts by the LG for a handoff. The RG dribbles in with a low left-hand dribble for a left-hand lay-up.

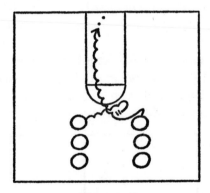

Diagram 3

4. Guard Button Hook Drill

Procedure:

(a) The RG breaks toward the basket and button hooks back to the free throw line where he stops quickly for a pass from the LG.

(b) The LG hits him with a pass and breaks off his left hip for a handoff and a right-hand lay-up.

(c) Work the drill with the LG becoming the pivot.

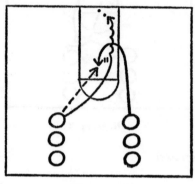

Diagram 4

5.   *Dribbling Roll out*

Procedure:

(a) The LG dribbles low with the right hand toward his RG's defensive man.

(b) When the LG gets two yards from the RG's man, the RG will foot-fake to his right and break off the right hip of the LG for a handoff.

(c) The LG will hand off, pivot backward on his left foot and start toward the goal looking over his left shoulder. The RG will take one dribble and stop quickly on both feet to bounce pass to the LG for a right hand lay-up.

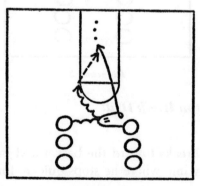

Diagram 5

B. *Guard to Forward Scoring Drills*

Guard to forward drills offer several potential methods of scoring. When the guard goes outside, he has a direct route to the basket. Every defensive man knows that it is difficult to keep from fouling this man if he drives well. The guard-to-forward pass is usually an easy one to make and in many offenses sets off a continuity of more complicated moves if the guard-to-forward options should fail. The drills shown here should be run to both sides of the floor.

6. Guard Inside Stationary Screen

Procedure:

(a) The RG passes to the RF and moves to set a screen on the forward's man.

(b) The RF foot fakes right and drives with the left hand for a left-hand lay-up on the far side of the basket.

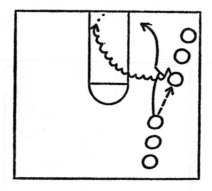

Diagram 6

7. Forward to Guard Inside Stationary Screen

Procedure:

(a) The RF passes to the RG and moves out to set a screen on the guard's man.

(b) The RG foot fakes to his left and drives right off the left hip of his screen man for a right-hand lay-up.

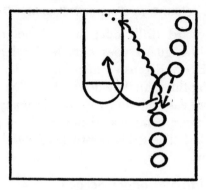

Diagram 7

8. Guard to Forward Roll out

Procedure:

(a) The RG passes to the RF and sets a one-count screen for him. He then pivots backward on his left foot, rolling toward the basket and looking over his left shoulder.

(b) The RG foot fakes right, recovers, and passes to the breaking guard so that he can receive and go up immediately for a right-hand lay-up.

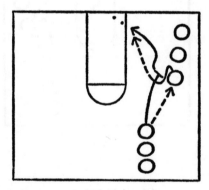

Diagram 8

9. Forward to Guard Roll out

Procedure:

(a) The RF passes to the RG and sets a one-count screen. The RF will then pivot backward on his right foot and break for the basket, looking over his right shoulder.

(b) The RG foot fakes left, recovers, and passes to the RF at a time that allows him to go up immediately for a right-hand lay-up.

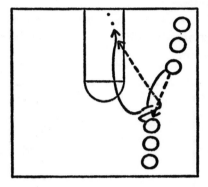

Diagram 9

10. *Guard to Forward Dribbling Screen*

Procedure:

(a) The RG dribbles low with the right hand toward the RF's defensive man.

(b) When the RG gets two yards from his defensive man, the RF foot-fakes right and breaks off the right hip of the RG for a handoff. The RF takes the handoff and dribbles with the left hand all the way to the far side of the basket for a left-hand lay-up.

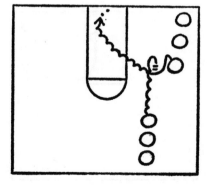

Diagram 10

11. Guard Outside Drill

Procedure:

(a) The RG passes to the RF and breaks outside off his left hip for a handoff.

(b) The RF makes the handoff and steps in front of the guard's defensive man while the RG is dribbling all the way for a right-hand lay-up.

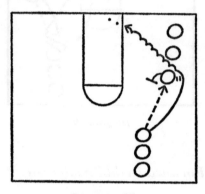

Diagram 11

12. Guard Hook Pass Drill

Procedure:

(a) The RG passes to the RF and breaks outside for the handoff.

(b) The RF makes the handoff and breaks for the basket, looking over his right shoulder.

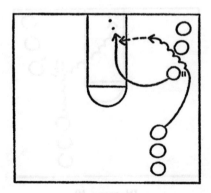

Diagram 12

(c) The RG makes a dribbling hook pass at a point where the RF can take the pass and go up for a right-hand lay-up.

13. *Forward to Guard Hook Pass Drill*

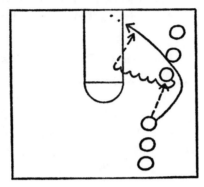

Diagram 13

Procedure:

(a) The RG passes to the RF and breaks outside for the handoff.

(b) The RF fakes the ball to the breaking RG and dribbles one time toward the free throw line. At this point the RF jumps for a hook pass to the RG, who has continued his break for the basket.

(c) The RG takes the pass and makes a right-hand lay-up.

14. *Guard Forward Pivot Drill*

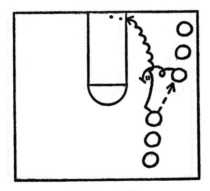

Diagram 14

Procedure:

(a) The RG passes to the RF. The RF steps toward the free throw line and takes a long dribble while doing so.

(b) The RG foot fakes left and drives off the left hip of the forward where he has stopped a yard from the key hole area.

(c) The RG takes the handoff and goes for the right-hand lay-up.

C. *Forward to Forward Drills*

Many offenses require the forwards to be able to play pivot. This has come about because so many opportunities present themselves for the forward to break into the pivot briefly for a scoring play. Some of the best of these opportunities come about as the result of passes and plays from forward to forward. It is understood that all of these drills are to be run to both sides of the floor.

15. *Forward to Forward Passing Drill*

Procedure:

(a) The LF breaks across the middle and receives a high pass from the RF in the key hole area.

(b) The LF takes the pass and continues on to the basket for a right-hand lay-up.

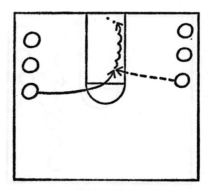

Diagram 15

16. *Forward to Forward Reverse Pivot Drill*

Procedure:

(a) The LF breaks into the free throw lane for a high pass from the RF.

(b) The LF takes the pass and stops at the same time. He pivots backward on his left foot and drives for a left-hand lay-up.

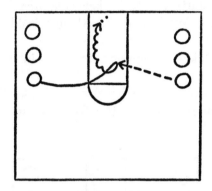

Diagram 16

17. *Forwards' Criss-Cross*

Procedure:

(a) The LF breaks into the key hole for a high pass from the RF. After receiving the pass, the LF stops immediately, facing center court.

(b) The RF follows his pass and breaks off the right hip of the LF for a handoff and driving left-hand lay-up.

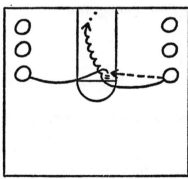 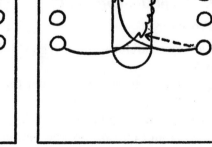

Diagram 17A   *Diagram 17B*

(c) Another option to this drill is to have the LF fake the handoff and pivot for a right-hand lay-up.

18. *Forward to Forward Dribbling Drill*

Procedure:

(a) The RF dribbles low with the left hand to the key hole area.

(b) The LF starts across the key hole area at the same time. He breaks off the left hip of the RF just inside the free throw line.

(c) The LF takes the handoff and goes in for the right-hand lay-up.

(d) Another option is to have the LF take the handoff and take a set or jump shot over the RF, who acts as a stationary screen.

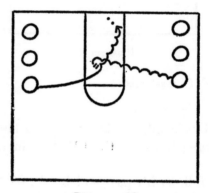

Diagram 18

D. *Forwards and Guards Pivot Cutting Drills*

19. *Pivot Handoff Drill*

Procedure:

(a) Place all forwards and guards behind their normal offensive spots.

(b) Place all pivot men under the basket with one pivot standing on the free throw line.

(c) Let each man in each of the four lines take a turn at hitting the pivot and cutting for the handoff. The cutter should always fake one way and cut the other. After taking the handoff he will go for the lay-up with that hand, which keeps the ball away from the imaginary defense. All pivot men take a turn on the spot.

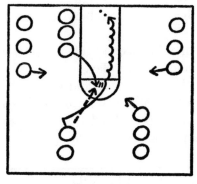

Diagram 19

20. *Pivot Fake and Turn Drill*

Procedure:

(a) Place all forwards and guards in their normal offensive positions with one pivot on the free throw line.

(b) The men in each of the four lines take turns hitting the pivot and breaking for a handoff.

(c) The pivot fakes the handoff and turns for the shot with the outside hand.

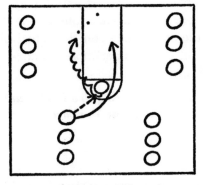

Diagram 20

21. *Pivot Screen Drill*

Procedure:

(a) Place all pivot men in a line under the basket, with one pivot standing on the free throw line.

(b) Put all other team members in one line at the right guard spot.

(c) The pivot man breaks and sets a screen where the guard's defensive man would usually play.

(d) The guard fakes one way and drives the other with that hand, which keeps the ball away from the defense.

(e) The line should be shifted frequently so that it operates from all offensive positions except the pivot.

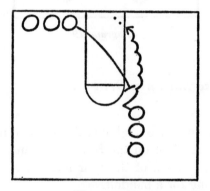

Diagram 21

II. Three Man Scoring Drills

Three-man drills offer almost as many opportunities for scoring as five-man situations offer. Most set plays or patterns will require one or more men to clear out a side or to "entertain" their men while the other three run the actual play. By breaking the offense down in this manner more practice can be had in a shorter period of time.

A. *Drills That Require Both Guards and One Forward*

22. *The Weave*

Procedure:

(a) Three lines of men are necessary for this drill. One line is placed behind each guard spot. Another line is placed behind the right forward position.

(b) The RG dribbles to the LG and sets an inside screen.

(c) The LG dribbles with the right hand to the inside of the RF, who breaks off his right hip for a handoff.

(d) The RF uses a low left-hand dribble and goes all the way in for a left-hand lay-up.

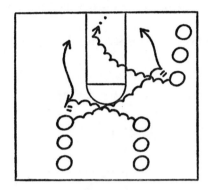

Diagram 22

23. *Opposite Guard Around Drill*

Procedure:

(a) The LF passes to the RG. The RG passes to the RF and goes inside to screen the RF's man, after which he rolls out to the base line.

(b) While the screen is being set, the RF uses a left-hand dribble and moves to the free throw line.

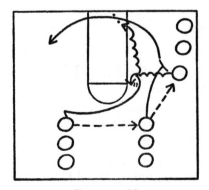

Diagram 23

(c) The LG fakes to the left and drives to his right off the left hip of the RF, who gives him a handoff. The LG takes the handoff and goes up for a right-hand lay-up.

24. *Outside Trailer Play Drill*

Procedure:

(a) The RG passes to the RF and breaks outside for the hand-off. He dribbles halfway to the corner and with a rear pivot faces in court.

(b) After handing off, the RF breaks across to the free throw line.

(c) The LG gives a head and shoulder fake to the left and breaks close behind the RF as the RF approaches the free throw line.

(d) The RG bounce passes to the breaking LG for a right-hand lay-up.

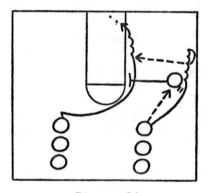

Diagram 24

25. *Guard Opposite Drill*

Procedure:

(a) The RG passes to the RF and breaks opposite to his LG and sets a screen for him.

(b) The LG breaks behind the screening RG and receives a pass from the RF as he breaks for the basket and a lay-up.

(c) A good option for this drill is to let the RF dribble toward the free throw line one dribble and face outward. From this position he gives a handoff to the LG breaking on his outside for a lay-up.

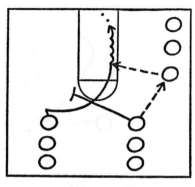 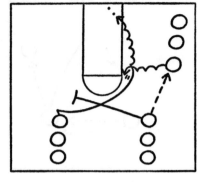

Diagram 25A   Diagram 25B

26. Three Man Continuity Drill

Procedure:

(a) The RG passes to the RF and breaks straight for the basket.

(b) The RF fakes a pass to him but passes out to the LG, who slides across to take the place of the RG. The breaking RG comes back to the spot which was originally occupied by the LG.

(c) The new RG passes to the new LG and breaks straight for the basket. The new LG fakes a pass to him but instead passes to the RF, who slides out to take the RG's spot. The breaking RG turns outward and slides into the RF spot.

(d) The drill will continue indefinitely in this manner.

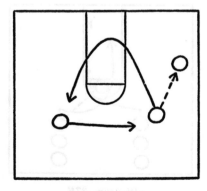 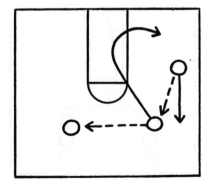

Diagram 26A   Diagram 26B

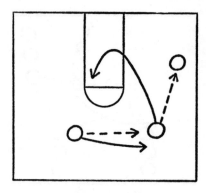

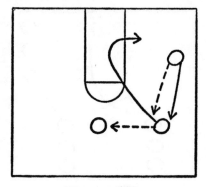

Diagram 26C   *Diagram 26D*

B. *Drills Involving Both Guards and the Pivot Man*

These drills will be recognized by all coaches as being various ways of splitting the post from the guard positions. To run these drills, line up all pivot men except one behind the basket. Place one pivot man on the free throw line and all other players in two lines, one behind each guard spot.

27. *Guard's Criss-Cross*

Procedure:

(a) The LG passes to the post man and breaks off the pivot's left hip.

(b) Almost simultaneously, the RG foot fakes to the right and breaks behind the LG and off the right hip of the pivot.

(c) The pivot can hand to either one of these men.

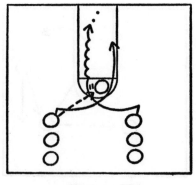

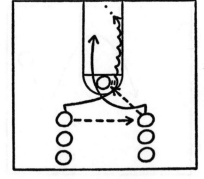

Diagram 27A   *Diagram 27B*

(d) A good variation to this drill is to have the ball passed from the LG to the RG, from which the criss-cross is worked in the same manner.

28. Guard Roll out Criss-Cross

Procedure:

(a) The LG passes to the RG and moves over to set a screen on the RG's defensive man. The RG passes the ball to the pivot, halting momentarily while the LG is pivoting rearward on his left foot to make his break for the basket.

(b) As soon as the LG pivots, the RG breaks behind him and off the right hip of the pivot man.

(c) The pivot man can hand to either cutter.

(d) An interesting option is to have the LG pass to the pivot, break to his right, screen for the RG and roll out for the basket. The play is then run the same as already described.

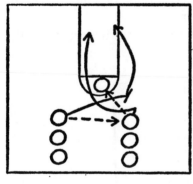 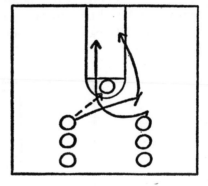

Diagram 28A   *Diagram 28B*

29. Dribbling Criss-Cross

Procedure:

(a) The LG dribbles toward the RG.

(b) At the same time the RG starts toward the dribbler and takes a handoff about half way between the two guard positions. After taking the handoff and using a left-hand outside hook pass, he passes to the pivot.

(c) Both players continue the break for the basket and the pivot man can hand to either one.

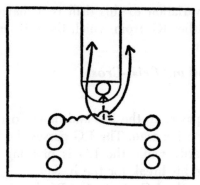

Diagram 29

30. Double Screen Shot Drill

Procedure:

(a) The LG passes to the pivot and breaks to the pivot's left hip, where he stops momentarily.

(b) The RG breaks to a point outside these two men where he receives a shovel pass from the pivot man.

(c) The RG can jump shoot or set shoot after receiving the pass.

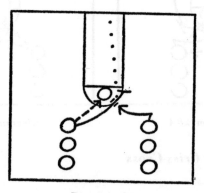

Diagram 30

C. Drills Involving One Guard, One Forward and the Pivot

These drills present various methods of splitting the post from the side. All guards can be placed behind the right guard position, all forwards are placed behind the right forward position. One pivot man is placed on the free throw line and the others behind the basket to await their turn.

31. Guard Forward Criss-Cross Drill

Procedure:

(a) The RG passes to the RF who passes to the pivot.

(b) Both players criss-cross off the pivot, with the RF going first.

(c) The pivot can hand to either player.

(d) One option to this drill is to have the RG pass to the pivot, from which both players will criss-cross, with the guard going first.

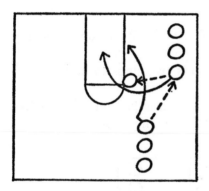 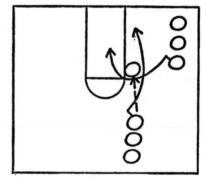

Diagram 31A   *Diagram 31B*

32. Roll out Criss-Cross

Procedure:

(a) The RF breaks out and sets his screen to the rear of the RG's defensive man.

(b) The RG passes to the pivot, fakes left and breaks right around the screen.

(c) As the right guard breaks, the right forward pivots to the rear on his right foot and breaks for the basket off the right hip of the pivot.

(d) The pivot man hands to either cutter.

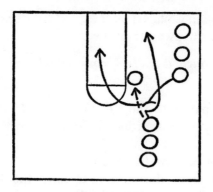

Diagram 32

33. *Pivot Screen Shot Drill*

Procedure:

(a) The RG passes to the RF.

(b) After making the pass, the RG breaks through the key hole lane and off the left hip of the pivot.

(c) The pivot fakes right and cuts two steps toward the RF, right behind the breaking RG.

(d) The RF hits the pivot with a pass just outside the free throw lane, where the pivot man takes a jump shot.

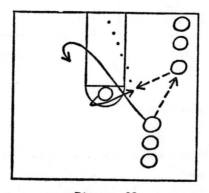

Diagram 33

34. *Forward Screen Shot Drill*

Procedure:

(a) The RG passes to the RF and breaks to a point just to the left of the pivot, where he stops for a dead screen.

(b) The RF receives the pass and passes to the pivot ahead of the moving guard.

(c) The pivot receives the pass and stands fast until the RF breaks to a point just outside the two men who are setting a stationary screen for his jump shot.

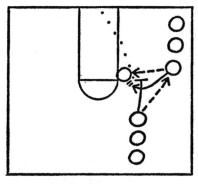

Diagram 34

35. Guard Outside Drill

Procedure:

(a) The RG passes to the RF and breaks for the basket outside the RF.

(b) The RF passes to the pivot and breaks for the basket outside of the pivot man.

(c) The pivot holds the ball until the RG reaches a point on the base line, where he takes the pass for a right hand lay-up.

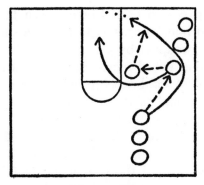

Diagram 35

36. *Guard Hook and Criss-Cross Drill*

Procedure:

(a) The RG passes to the RF and breaks to the outside for a handoff. He takes one dribble and pivots inward on his left foot, facing the pivot man.

(b) The RF, after taking the handoff, breaks out to the spot formerly occupied by the RG. Here he pivots backward on his right foot facing the man with the ball.

(c) At this point the RG bounce passes to the pivot and follows the pass, breaking off the right hip of the pivot.

(d) The RF fakes left and breaks right behind the breaking RG to take the handoff from the pivot for a right hand lay-up.

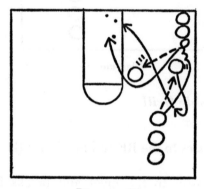

Diagram 36

37. *Three Man Continuity Series*

Procedure:

(a) Player #1 passes to #2 and breaks straight for the basket. #2 fakes a pass to him but passes to #3, who slides out to take the spot formerly occupied by #1.

(b) The breaking guard moves into the vacated pivot spot.

(c) #2 passes to #3 and breaks straight for the basket. #3 fakes a pass to him but instead passes to #1, who moves over to take the vacated right forward spot. #2 takes #1's place.

(d) #3, after passing to #1, breaks for the basket and #1 fakes a pass to him but passes back to #2. #2 comes to #3's spot to receive the ball. #1 breaks toward the goal while #2 fakes to him and passes to #3. #2 breaks for the goal as #3 passes to #1 and breaks. At this point all the men are in their original places.

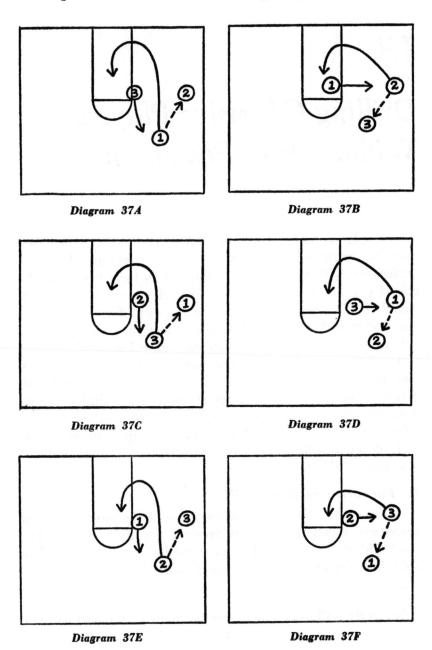

Diagram 37A   Diagram 37B

Diagram 37C   Diagram 37D

Diagram 37E   Diagram 37F

13

Drilling Offensive Players Without Ball Possession

Some players appear to be of all-American calibre when they gain ball possession. These same players sometimes look like novices when they do not have the ball in their hands. In the offensive court, where there are five offensive ball players, it would seem to be obvious that the majority of action involves movements without the ball. It is extremely important for individuals to know what to do when they are being tightly pressed by the defensive player. It is important for the pivot man to know how to get open for receipt of a pass. It is important for all players to know how to run a screen route. Many drills covering these situations can be found in other chapters. However, the following drills are inserted for the specific purpose of impressing each player with the importance of knowing what to do without possession of the ball.

1. Forward Receiving Drill

In the normal single post offense, one of the most important movements involved is the sure accurate pass from guard to forward. This drill is designed to teach the forward how to evade a tight defender and receive the guard's pass cleanly.

Procedure:

(a) Station all front men in one line behind a forward position, and all guards in one line behind the guard spot on that side of the floor. The forwards take turns as receivers and defenders.

(b) The first guard dribbles and comes to a halt about three steps from the head of the circle. The first forward fakes two steps toward the base line and breaks back for receipt of the guard's pass.

(c) If the forward's defender is still with him as he breaks forward and stretches to meet the pass, he turns quickly and cuts straight and fast for the basket and a lay-up.

(d) The guard tries to hit him on his initial break, but if this is impossible, he delays the pass and hits him on his cut down the base line.

(e) Each performer moves to the rear of his respective group.

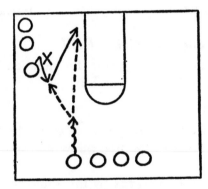

Diagram 1

2. *Forward Cut Off Screen*

The best screen becomes valueless unless the player receiving the screen deploys himself properly. This drill teaches forwards how to break into the pivot area after having received a screen set by the pivot.

Procedure:

(a) Arrange the squad in three lines as shown in the diagram.

(b) The first man in line 2 breaks out to set a screen just to the left of the free throw line. The first player in line 1 fakes left and cuts tight off the screen man's left hip for a pass from the first player of line 3.

(c) All performers change lines after each performance. An

extra defensive man may be added to the drill to make it more
gamelike, as shown in Diagram 2b.

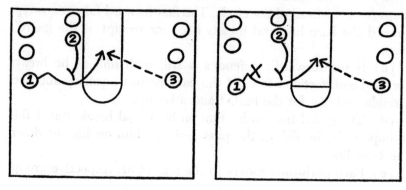

| Diagram 2A | Diagram 2B |

3. Guard to Guard Receiving Drill

This drill will prepare the guards for situations where the defense presses the receiver very tightly.

Procedure:

(a) Place all players in three lines as shown by Diagram 3.

(b) Player #2 fakes to the free throw line and breaks back to
receive #1's pass.

(c) If #2 has not evaded #2x by this time, he will fake to the
center line and break back through the key hole for the pass. All
players exchange lines.

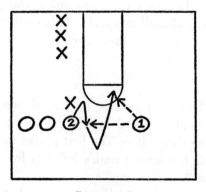

Diagram 3

4. Guard Cut off Screen

This drill teaches the guard how to rub his defender off on a stationary screen.

Procedure:

(a) Place a group of forwards in the corner. Put all guards in line behind the left guard spot. The pivot men act as screen men in the middle line.

(b) The first guard fakes left and cuts right off the stationary screen.

(c) The first forward passes to him as he clears the screen.

(d) A defensive player can be added, as shown in Diagram 4b.

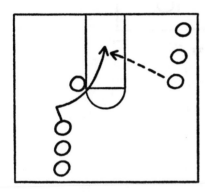 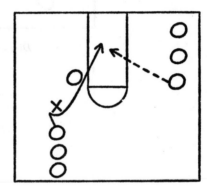

Diagram 4A   *Diagram 4B*

5. Pivot Screening Drill

In many offensive systems, the pivot must be able to screen. The following drill is designed to help teach this skill.

Procedure:

(a) Place all guards and forwards in regular single post offensive position.

(b) Allow one member of each line to act as a defensive player.

(c) Place one pivot man in the pivot area with a defensive player.

(d) On a signal from the coach, the pivot moves and screens for any of the four other players.

(e) The person receiving the screen cuts for the basket. The pivot rolls out in case of a defensive switch.

(f) The coach passes to either player who is open for the shot.

(g) The pivot will alternate by screening for a different line each time.

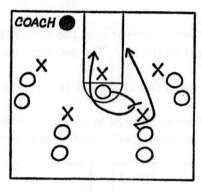

Diagram 5

Part III

DRILLS FOR TEACHING DEFENSIVE FUNDAMENTALS

No matter how successful a team becomes offensively, there comes a time when it will win or lose according to its defensive ability. Everyone has heard the saying, "the best defense is a good offense." However, if we can score as often as we want to and have no defense, it will amount to nothing but trading buckets. This is no way to win consistently. The defensive game should be given just as much time and effort as the offensive game. If a player scores only two points and holds his man scoreless, he has had a successful night. The difference in the number of points scored by a player and his opponent is more important than individual point totals. A player has not contributed much to the team's cause if he scores twenty points and allows his opponent to score twenty-five.

Defense can be fun. A great sense of satisfaction can be obtained from playing good defense. Few boys have experienced the thrill of holding a "big gun" to three or four points. It is this achievement that separates the men from the boys.

A team must recognize the coach's intention not to compromise with good defensive play. The team must develop defensive pride. Statistics can be of value in selling this part of basketball. A team has good defense when its members begin to vie for the honor of guarding the opposing team's hotshot.

Good defensive play is the result of team unity in employing individual skills. Stages of progression include individual drills, two and three man drills, and team drills. Stance and footwork are the most important aspects of teaching individual defensive skill. A good stance is one with the knees bent, feet spread well apart and with one foot slightly forward, and the arms up. One arm should be raised toward the opponent and the other arm should be raised sideward. The body should be bent forward at the waist with the weight of the body distributed evenly on both feet. If the offensive man starts a cut or drive the weight shifts to the rear foot. The first step backward is taken with the rear foot. The first step is always taken with the foot nearest the direction of the opponent's drive. The feet slide step without allowing the legs to cross. This procedure is used in the scoring area. On full or sometimes on half court breaks, it is necessary to run straight and hard to a point where the offensive man can be safely intercepted.

Two and three man drills are used chiefly to learn how to switch or slide with your teammates while using the good fundamental footwork described. Team drills have the same purpose.

14

Drills to Develop Individual Defensive Ability

1. Boxer's Footwork Drill

The footwork used by boxers is ideal for defensive basketball. This drill can be practiced by the entire team. A short period of time will give most boys a good workout.

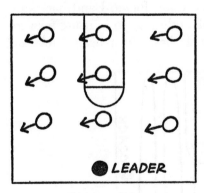

Diagram 1A   Diagram 1B

Procedure:

(a) Arrange the squad on one end of the floor as shown in

Diagram 1. Each player should have plenty of space in which to move.

(b) The coach will signal right, left, forward and backward by pointing. One of the players may perform this function.

(c) The team responds by moving in the direction that has been signaled. Close supervision should be given to the footwork of each athlete. The feet should never be crossed at any time during this drill.

(d) For a variation have the team respond to a dribbler.

2. *Defensive Footwork Relay*

Winners of this type of relay should properly take pride in their ability to move fast without crossing the feet. They will become better defensive players as a result.

Procedure:

(a) Put every player in position straddling the center line, with everyone facing the same direction.

(b) On a signal from the coach, every man slide steps to his right until he can reach out and touch the wall with his right hand. Then he slides back to center line moving to his left. The first man back is the winner and is eliminated. Keep running the same drill until the slowest man is found. This should provide incentive for the slower men to work on defensive footwork.

(c) Run the same type of relay using forward and backward steps. Have the team face the wall and move to it, using forward slide steps. When they reach the wall they return, using backward

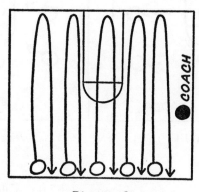

Diagram 2

slide steps. Continue to run the drill until the slowest man is found.

3. *Feel for the Screen Drill*

Those players who get out of screens most often are continuously feeling for possible screeners moving up on them from the side or the rear. This drill will help instill the habit.

Procedure:

(a) Place ten chairs at random anywhere on the floor.

(b) Arrange the squad at one end of the gymnasium in five lines.

(c) The first five men turn their backs to the opposite end of the floor. On the coach's signal they move out toward the other end using backward sliding defensive footwork.

(d) It is obvious that these men will have to be constantly feeling for those chairs to keep from backing into them. Be sure that no one turns his head more than about twenty degrees. A method of checking on this is to have the team return to position if the coach should suddenly raise his arm. Those who miss the signal have not been using proper split vision.

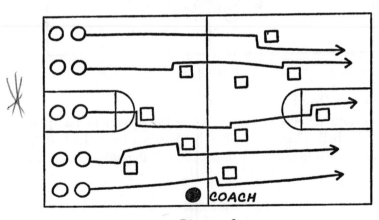

Diagram 3

4. *Stance in Motion Drill*

This drill will help impress the players with the importance of keeping a good defensive stance at all times. (Good stance and footwork are described in the introduction to this section.)

Procedure:

(a) Have the team pair off by twos.

(b) So that the coach can supervise better, have each pair face each other across the center line.

(c) Each boy in each pair drops into a good defensive stance and one line is designated as the *leaders.*

(d) On the coach's signal, the leaders move in any direction they desire. They must use good footwork. The other line, or *followers,* imitate the same footwork and direction.

(e) After the drill has been run in this way for a short time, allow the other line to become the leaders.

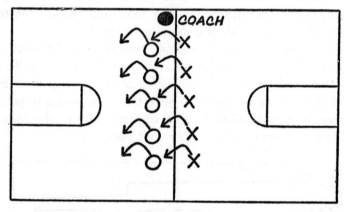

Diagram 4

5. *One on One Position Drill*

Some boys defend very well while the opponent has possession of the ball. They relax when he does not have the ball. This drill is designed to teach the importance of defending at *all* times.

Procedure:

(a) Put one line of men in a corner as defensive players. Place another line of offensive players behind the forward spot on the same side of the floor.

(b) The coach stands on the opposite side of the floor with a ball.

(c) Players #1 and #2 compete first. Good defensive position should be maintained at all times by #2. #1 tries to maneuver for offensive position anywhere on the same end of the floor. If

#1 obtains an advantage by position on #2, the coach will pass the ball to #1 for an attempt at the basket.

(d) After a short while, if no advantage is gained by #1, the next two men in the lines will take their turn. #1 and #2 will exchange lines. The positions for starting the drill can be altered as the coach desires.

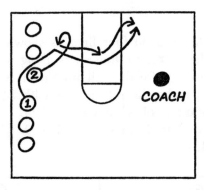

Diagram 5

6. *Defensive Circle Drill*

The circle drill provides a method of learning how to switch quickly from offense to defense.

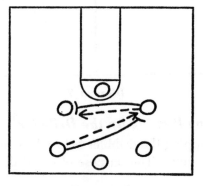

Diagram 6

Procedure:

(a) Place six men in a circle.

(b) Any player can start the drill. He passes to another player and follows the pass to guard the receiver. The receiver passes by him to another player and follows the pass to guard that receiver.

(c) Several circles of men may run this drill simultaneously.

7. Slide Step Drill

The purpose of this drill is to develop the ability to slide step and defense at the same time.

Procedure:

(a) Station the team in four lines as shown on the diagram.

(b) #1 dribbles to #3. #3 slide steps along with #1 facing his right side and reaching for the ball any time it is not protected.

(c) #2 and #4 make the return trip with #4 facing #2's left side while he slide steps back down the floor.

(d) #1 goes to line 4. #3 goes to line 2. #2 goes to line 3. #4 goes to line 1.

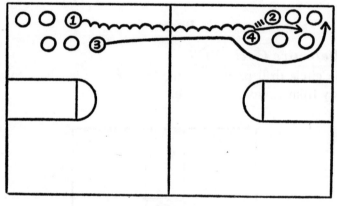

Diagram 7

8. One on One Picking up the Dribbler

The art of stopping the dribbler before he reaches his objective is of great importance. The purpose of this drill is to develop this skill.

Procedure:

(a) Divide the squad into two lines. Place one line at a free throw line and the other line at the opposite end of the gym.

(b) The first man on the free throw line starts dribbling toward the other goal.

(c) The first man on that end moves out to pick him up just as he crosses center line. The defensive man tries, by faking and retreating, to force the dribbler to a halt before he reaches his position. The coach tells each dribbler as he moves out where he wants the dribbler to go if possible.

(d) The dribbler can always drive by the defensive man and go for a lay-up if the defensive boy over commits himself.

(e) The lines will alternate.

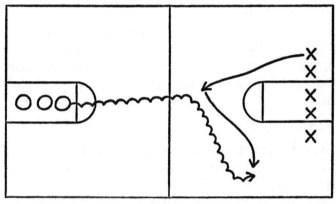

Diagram 8

9. Drill to Force the Dribbler Inside

Most coaches feel that if the dribbler is forced inside there is less likelihood of the dribbler going all the way. This drill will help cultivate this habit among the players.

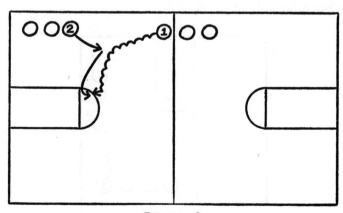

Diagram 9

Procedure:

(a) Divide the squad into two lines and station them as shown on the diagram.

(b) #1 starts dribbling from the center side line.

(c) #2 moves out to meet him. #2 will *show* the dribbler the inside without giving any definite advantage either way.

(d) Run this drill from varying angles. Have the men exchange lines after each performance.

10. Head on Drill

Some players will turn sideways at the last minute if the dribbler makes a really aggressive drive. This means that if there is contact, the responsibility is placed on the defensive man. This drill is designed to prevent this type of "panty-waist" defensive reaction.

Procedure:

(a) Two lines are placed near a side line and facing each other.

(b) #1 starts dribbling down the side line and #2 moves to intercept him.

(c) When #1 gets two paces from #2, #2 will place his left foot solidly on the side line. Allow #1 to make solid contact with #2 so that #2 will learn that this contact is something that every real athlete can withstand. In doing so he will learn that the free throw he gains is much better than turning sideways and hooking the dribbler.

(d) Each player will exchange lines, and the drill should be run on the other side of the floor.

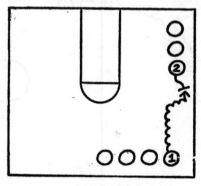

Diagram 10

11. Drill to Avoid Being Screened

Certain players seem to be able to slide or roll out of every screen. Others always appear to get trapped. Part of this is inherent. A good part can be learned.

Procedure:

(a) Place all guards behind the left guard position. All forwards are put behind the left toward slot. The remaining post men will form a line under the basket, except for the first one. He assumes a defensive stance in front of the first forward.

(b) #1 passes to #2 and moves inside to set a screen on #3. #2 tries to use the screen by faking the base line and driving over the back of the screener and to the free throw area for a shot.

(c) #3 makes every effort to roll around the screen, cause the screener to *miss*, or to slide by the screener and stay with his man.

(d) After each performance, the three lines rotate in a clockwise manner to the next line.

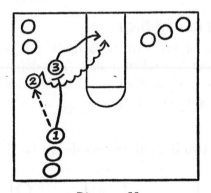

Diagram 11

12. Hand Deflection Drill

The dribbler will occasionally gain a half step advantage on the defensive player. If this happens, the defensive player should not force the play by hooking or fouling; he should get in step with the dribbler and try to deflect the shot as the lay-up is attempted. The purpose of this drill is to work on such situations.

Procedure:

(a) Arrange the squad in two lines as shown on the diagram.

(b) Player #1 purposely gives #2 a half step break on him toward the basket down the base line.

(c) #1 falls in step with #2 and tries to deflect or block the lay-up attempt.

(d) #1 and #2 will exchange lines. Work the drill from varying positions on the floor.

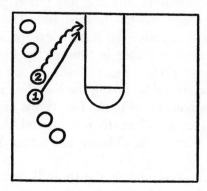

Diagram 12

13. *Rebound Cut off Drill*

The objective of this drill is to teach the proper maneuvers after an opponent has taken a shot. The defensive man should turn toward the goal, looking over his shoulder to keep himself between the shooter and the goal.

Procedure:

(a) Position two lines of men as shown by the diagram.

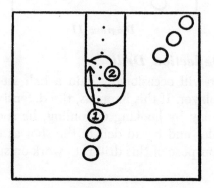

Diagram 13

(b) #1 shoots and moves for the rebound. #2 will also move for the goal but he will make sure to keep himself between #1 and the rebound.

(c) #1 and #2 will swap lines.

14. Halting the Dribbler with Two on One

When a defensive man is caught with two men forcing him for a lay-up he must halt the dribbler. This drill will help instill the proper habits when he is faced with such a dilemma.

Procedure:

(a) Post three lines as shown by the diagram.

(b) #1 starts to dribble down the middle toward #3. When #1 gets a step from the head of the free throw circle, #3 moves out to halt him.

(c) After stopping the dribbler, #3 drops off fast to check #2. The players exchange lines. For a good option, have #2 come down the other side line.

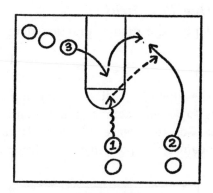

Diagram 14

15. Two Ball Press Drill

The purpose of this drill is to give the defensive player practice against a dribbler determined to go all the way.

Procedure:

(a) Place the squad in lines stationed at each corner of the floor.

(b) #2 moves down the floor to pick up #1 and presses him all the way. #3 moves down the floor to pick up #4 and press him.

#2 and #3 retrieve the rebounds, pass to the offensive lines and take their places in those lines. The offensive players go to the defensive lines.

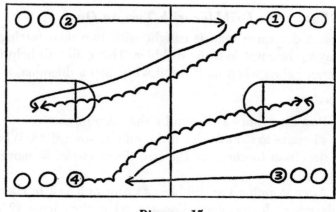

Diagram 15

16. Two on One Post Drill

This drill will give the guards practice sloughing off on the post man.

Procedure:

(a) Arrange the squad in six lines as shown on the diagram.

(b) #1 passes to #3 and stands still. Defensive man #2x immediately drops back to a place where he is virtually standing with his back against the post man, #3. Defensive player #3x

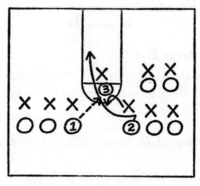

Diagram 16

crowds #3 from behind. These two defensive men attempt to tie up #3 so that he cannot break or make a handoff while #2 is cutting by.

17. Three on One Defensive Drill

The likelihood of defending this situation successfully is truly small. However, it is smaller still when the defensive man has never drilled for such an occasion.

Procedure:

(a) Arrange the squad in four lines. (See Diagram 18.)

(b) The middle man dribbles toward the defensive man as his cutters precede him slightly.

(c) The defensive man halts the dribbler and drops back directly under the basket.

(d) The defensive man will then have to take the cutter who receives the pass. By feinting and retreating he may cause a bad pass to be thrown or a fumbled receipt of the pass. He should show as much sign of aggressiveness as possible in an attempt to rattle the middle man.

(e) Rotate all lines.

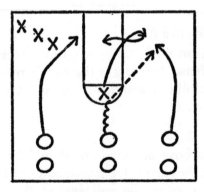

Diagram 17

18. Defensing the Post Man

The purpose of this drill is to give the defensive pivot man practice in positioning.

Procedure:

(a) Put one man at each of the guard and forward spots. Put

a post man in the key hole area and place a line of defensive post men under the goal, with the first one assigned to guard the post man.

(b) The offensive players move a ball back and forth or around the semi-circle while the post men jockey for position.

(c) For an added attraction, allow the offensive player to take one lap if the defensive man deflects the pass. Let the defensive man take a lap if the offensive man scores.

(d) The offensive and defensive post men exchange spots often.

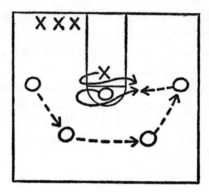

Diagram 18

19. Drilling for the Press

Conditioning is of vital importance to the team which expects to play good defense. Pressing is the most strenuous type of defense. Here is a drill to teach defensive tactics and develop good physical condition.

Procedure:

(a) Place two boys of equal speed and height on the free throw line. All other players are paired and waiting their turn.

(b) The coach tosses the ball against the backboard. Both boys go for the ball. The one who gains possession becomes the offensive dribbler and the other one becomes the presser.

(c) The dribbler tries to go to the other end and score. When he shoots it is a free ball again. The player who gets it is the offensive player and breaks for the other end of the floor to attempt a shot. The ball is free on each shot whether it goes in the basket or rebounds. Also, the defensive player may steal it at any time.

(d) These two players continue until one of them scores six points. Then two new men take their places.

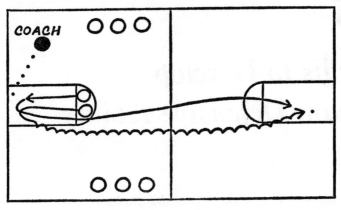

Diagram 19

15

Drills to Develop Team Defensive Ability

1. Two on Two Practicing the Switch

Some coaches demand that their players switch on defense. Some demand that they slide. Others want them to be able to do either. Possibly the best defensive teams can do both. The purpose of this drill is to practice the switch.

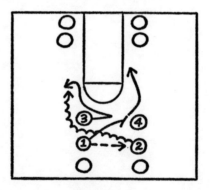

Diagram 1

Procedure:

(a) Arrange the squad in lines as shown on Diagram 1.

(b) #1 and #2 can work any number of the guard to guard offensive options while #3 and #4 practice the switch each time they cross.

(c) Rather than have the man in trouble call "switch," let both of them yell the switch loudly and push each other into switch position.

(d) Rotation from the offensive to the defensive lines is necessary so that everyone gets to practice this maneuver.

2. Two on Two Practicing the Slide

The purpose of this drill is to teach players how to cooperate while sliding by the screen to keep good defensive position.

Procedure:

(a) Four lines are arranged as shown in Diagram 2.

(b) #1 and #2 try any of the guard to guard options while #3 and #4 attempt to stay with the assigned man at all times. To slide, go behind the screen or between the screen and the goal. This opens up the possibility briefly for a set shot but that is better than opening up the opportunity for a lay-up.

(c) The defensive players should cooperate by stepping slightly backward to let the teammate by who is about to be picked.

(d) After the drill is run for a time in this manner, change the lines so that the defensive men become offensive and vice-versa.

(e) Run the guard to forward options in this way for practicing the slide also.

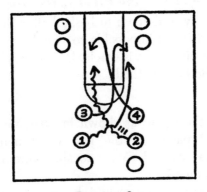

Diagram 2

3. Guard Forward Switching Drill

This is a situation where some teams switch and some teams slide. For those who switch, here is a drill to help beat the offense.

Procedure:

(a) Arrange the team in four lines as shown on the diagram.

(b) #1 passes to #2 and goes outside for the handoff and a drive for the bucket. #2x will take player #1 and #1x will take player #2.

(c) For practice on the other option in this situation, have #1 go inside and screen for #2. The switch still occurs but #2x must drift and play it considerably more loosely.

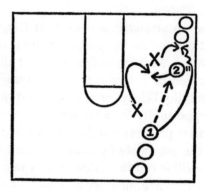

Diagram 3

4. Drill for Defensing the Pivot Criss-Cross

The hardest play to defense in basketball is the double cut off the pivot. It is virtually impossible to switch unless the switch is made before the pivot man is reached. Sliding is also difficult but appears to be the best method.

Procedure:

(a) Arrange the squad as shown in Diagram 4.

(b) #1 or #2 passes to the first pivot man from line 3. Defensive players #4 and #5 try to slide through with #1 and #2 as they cross off #3.

(c) The defensive men should be encouraged to use their hands on this drill to push their teammates on through the jam.

(d) The same defensive play needs to be practiced from the guard to forward pivot cross and can be done simply by changing the lines slightly.

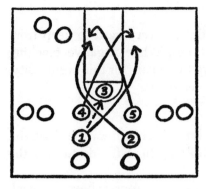 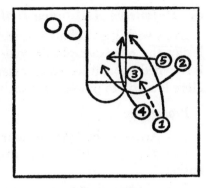

Diagram 4A   *Diagram 4B*

5. *Switching on a Single Cutter off Post*

The defensive post man will sometimes help a teammate by picking up a cutter who has gained a step on the teammate. The purpose of this drill is to develop such ability and cooperation between guards and pivot men.

Procedure:

(a) Arrange the team in four lines as shown in the diagram.

(b) #1 passes to #2 and cuts off his left hip. #4 steps half a step left to pick up the cutter without completely leaving his own man. After #3 has moved to #2's right and behind him, #4 leaves his man completely to take the cutter.

(c) Run this drill from the right guard spot also.

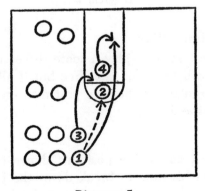

Diagram 5

6. Defensive Assistance Drill

Even with great effort put forth, it is very hard to keep from losing the offensive player sometimes. While negative teaching is frowned upon, it seems necessary to prepare for this eventuality. Here is a drill to practice for such occasions.

Procedure:

(a) Arrange the team in four lines as shown on the diagram.

(b) #1x allows his man to dribble by his left side toward the basket.

(c) #2x sees that an unguarded man is approaching the goal, so he shifts to take the new man. #2x still watches his own man out of the corner of his eye. He does everything possible to keep the two men from scoring.

(d) All lines rotate in a clockwise fashion.

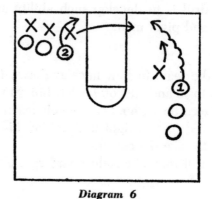

Diagram 6

7. Post Man Assist Play

One of the best men to play a loose driver is the defensive post man. This will leave his man free but if all defensive men are instructed to take the offensive post man on such occasions, it will minimize the danger.

Procedure:

(a) Place the team in the positions shown on the diagram.

(b) #1x allows his man to break down the base line. When #2x sees this driver he leaves his man completely and goes to the base line to try to get the driver to charge him.

(c) #1x moves quickly to take the free offensive post man.

(d) Rotate the lines but allow the post men to stay in that area.

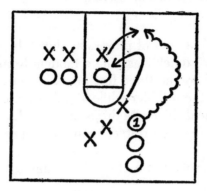

Diagram 7

8. *Out of Bounds Drill*

Some teams, when pressing, will allow both guards to take the man in bounds. All other men will be sticking with their opponents in an attempt to keep the out of bounds man from finding a receiver.

Procedure:

(a) Station lines of men as shown in the diagram.

(b) The out of bounds man tries to hit his teammate while the two defensive men try to prevent the pass.

(c) All lines rotate clockwise.

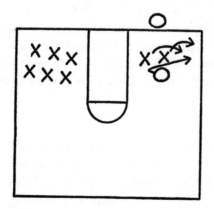

Diagram 8

9. Three on Two Defensive Drill

The purpose of this drill is to give the men practice for situations where they are outnumbered.

Procedure:

(a) Station five lines of players as shown by Diagram 9.

(b) #4 and #5 quickly assume a tandem formation when they are approached by the three fast break players.

(c) #4 halts the dribbler while #5 takes the cutter on his side. After halting the dribbler, #4 drops back quickly to take the other cutter. This leaves the dribbler with nothing to do with the ball but shoot.

(d) All lines rotate in a clockwise manner.

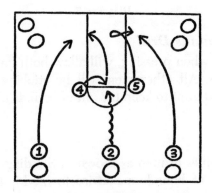

Diagram 9

10. Switching Against Three Men

Teams who employ the three out and two in offense will often run the three out in a weave offense. Unless the three defensive players are prepared to switch or slide properly, this offense can be quite dangerous. Here is a method of drilling for such an offense.

Procedure:

(a) Place the squad in six lines as shown by the diagram.

(b) The three offensive players attempt to cross and re-cross to shake one of the defensive men. The defensive men switch on every cross, calling the switch and pushing each other into position with their hands.

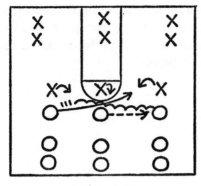

Diagram 10

(c) Each performer will swap lines with the man who faced him originally.

11. *Full Court Press Drill*

The purpose of this drill is twofold. One is to develop a full court pressing defense. The other is to develop circulo-respiratory endurance.

Procedure:

(a) Divide the squad into groups of five. Station one group in defensive positions and the other in offensive positions.

(b) The coach stands under the goal and makes a lay-up. The defensive team grabs the ball and takes it out of bounds. The

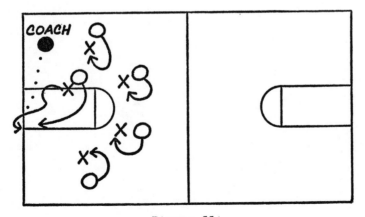

Diagram 11

offensive men turn to find their individual opponents and start the full court press. Two new groups will take their place and each group alternates after its performance so that everyone gets the same amount of practice.

Part IV

TACTICAL SITUATION DRILLS

Many basketball games are won by well-planned, well-practiced reactions to tactical situations. Conversely, many games are lost as a result of poorly organized reactions to the same situations. Through too much organization we may reach a point of diminishing returns when no opportunity is left for the youngsters to use their own natural initiative. However, something planned and practiced gives young men a sense of confidence that is often lacking when all play-making is left up to the players.

There are many situations in basketball that may be considered tactical. Some would say that the entire game is tactical, from the time when the team enters the dressing room until the game is over. Certainly all the preceding material on warm-ups, offense and defense could be placed in this category. We are going to offer drills concerned with three game conditions in this section. They are the jump ball, out of bounds and freeze situations. The free throw should also be considered in this category, and drills for the free throw situation are found in Chapter 4, "Shooting Drills." The free throw, jump ball and out of bounds situations should be worked into the daily practice schedule of every team. The freeze situation need not be rehearsed as often but cannot be left unpracticed. Careful statistics have proved that as many points are scored from these parts of the game as are scored from what we consider the normal offensive play. An effective approach to these situations will stamp a team as one that is well drilled. It is an approach that lifts the team from the good to the great category. It is an approach which increases player respect for the coach.

16

Jump Ball Drills

The jump ball situation occurs too often in a game to ignore. A team doesn't have to be the tallest to maintain the advantage at the jump, but it certainly helps. After a ball is tipped, it is free for anyone to secure possession. Many short teams concede those tips and others seem to get the ball as often as the team that actually has more height. Simply making the team conscious of the importance of the jump ball situation will increase the number of times possession is gained. A better method is to have some plan and to drill on it each practice day.

1. Sargent Jump

The purpose of this drill is to develop pride in each boy concerning his ability to jump.

Procedure:

(a) Place a blackboard with the lower edge at head-height and extending vertically upward.

(b) A player extends his arm and makes a chalk mark at the highest point to which he can reach while standing close to the wall. He then squats and jumps as high as he can, at which point he makes another mark.

(c) The distance between the two marks is measured. Each player is given an opportunity to make this attempt. Anything over twenty-four inches is quite good.

2. *Four Man Jumping Drill*

The purpose of this drill is to give the players practice in making the tap *to* a teammate.

Procedure:

(a) Arrange the team in groups of four around the gym floor.

(b) Each group is given a ball. One player in each group starts the drill by tossing the ball overhead and tapping it to a teammate. The drill moves continuously with each person jumping to meet the ball and tapping it to another man.

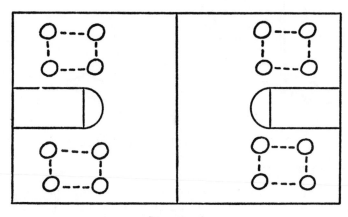

Diagram 2

3. *Vault Standard Drill*

This drill is similar to the Sargent Jump in that its main purpose is to instill jumping pride. It also makes jumping more interesting to the boys.

Procedure:

(a) Place a set of vaulting standards at the edge of the gym floor. Put the cross bar at ten feet.

(b) Allow every boy to try to touch the cross bar at that height.

(c) Raise the bar three inches higher and give every player another chance. Continue to make three-inch raises until only one man is left who can touch the bar. He is declared the winner.

Sketch for Drill #3. Vault Standard Drill.

4. Board Tipping Drill

Here is another drill used primarily to develop jumping consciousness and pride in jumping ability. It also develops stronger fingers and wrists for tipping.

Procedure:

(a) Secure a ten foot length of one-inch pipe at a height of thirteen feet from the floor.

(b) Six pieces of 2" x 4" board are needed, varying in length from 1'2" to 4'2", with intervals of six inches in between each piece. Holes are bored in each piece two inches from one end and by means of these the boards are slid along the pipe so that they hang at heights of from nine feet to twelve feet, with one-half foot graduation between each board. (See Sketch #4.)

(c) Each player takes a turn tipping at these boards until he finds the highest point of his jump. He then practices daily at that board. He should tip the board hard enough to cause it to revolve all the way around the pipe.

Sketch for Drill #4. Board Tipping Drill.

5. Three Man Tapping Drill

This drill more closely resembles the game situation. It is a method of practicing the tap.

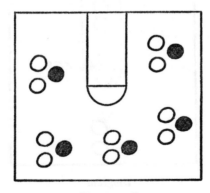

Diagram 5

Procedure:

(a) Place the team in groups of three, with one man in each group designated as the referee.

(b) The referee of each group tosses while the other two players practice tapping at the ball.

(c) The referee duties rotate among players so that all three have a chance to practice tapping.

6. *Two Line Drill*

This is a drill to develop timing, position for jumping, and control of the tip.

Procedure:

(a) Arrange the squad in two lines. The lines face each other across one of the floor circles. Each pair of jumpers should be of comparable height.

(b) Let a manager toss the ball between the first two jumpers at a height beyond either one's jumping ability. Each jumper tries to make the tip.

(c) The jumpers take their places at the end of the same line and the next two men move into position.

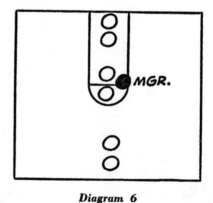

Diagram 6

7. *Tipping and Receiving Drill*

Receiving cannot be overlooked. It is just as important as jumping. This drill is designed to develop determined receiving of the tip.

Procedure:

(a) Arrange a formation at a circle as shown by Diagram 7.

(b) #1, #3, and #5 are on the same team. #2, #4, and #6 are working together.

(c) #1 tries to tip to #5, and #4 will try to tip to #2. #3 and #6 try to intercept if their teammates should fail to get off a good tip.

(d) #3 goes to the end of the line behind #4. #6 goes to the end of the line behind #1. All other men rotate one notch counter-clockwise except #7 and #8, who simply step forward one pace.

(e) The drill can be altered to have the tippers tip in any direction while other men are designated as interceptors.

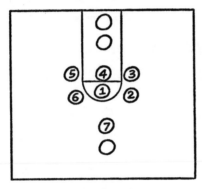

Diagram 7

8. *Clock Jump Ball Drill*

This drill helps teach the jumper to control his tip and gives his teammates the advantage of knowing where to go for the ball.

Procedure:

(a) Divide the squad into "giants" and "midgets" by putting all the tallest men in one line. The other line of shorties face them across a floor circle.

(b) The tall jumper who starts the drill will call the direction of his tip before he jumps. He calls any hour of the day from one to twelve. He assumes that the circle is a clock face, with twelve o'clock straight ahead of him and six o'clock directly behind him. The other hour directions are arranged accordingly.

(c) The jumper then tries to tip in the direction he has called. This enables receivers to gain possession of the tip more often.

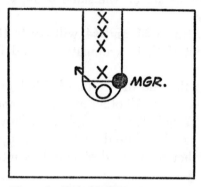

Diagram 8

9. Defensive Jump Ball Drill

This drill involves a gamble that most extremely short teams would be willing to make.

Procedure:

(a) Place two teams of five men each at one of the floor circles.

(b) When the ball is tipped by player #5x, who is much taller than #5, all of 5's teammates rotate. #1 moves to his right to a point one step from #2x. #2 moves between #2x and #3x. #3 moves only slightly to his right between #3x and 4x. #4 stays with his man.

(c) These movements leave #1x virtually unguarded. This is a

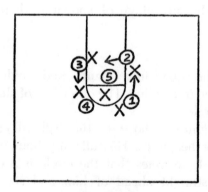

Diagram 9

calculated risk. It is a percentage risk because few boys can tip well to their right rear if they are right handed. This gamble places one and one-fourth men on each of 5x's receivers.

10. *Diamond Scoring Drill*

There are many scoring drills that can be used by a team that can control the tap. Here is a basic formation from which many drills can be worked.

Procedure:

(a) A strong jumper is placed in the jumping circle. A tall, strong boy is placed in front of him outside the circle. The other men are arranged as wing men and one safety man.

(b) The jumper taps the ball, tossed by the coach, to the man facing him. This player passes to one of the wing men as they break for the goal.

(c) If the regular receiver of the tap is crowded, the jumper may tap hard and directly to either of the wing men.

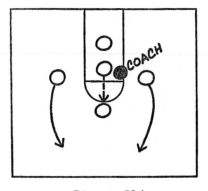
Diagram 10A

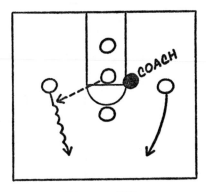
Diagram 10B

11. *Rectangular Scoring Drills*

This traditional formation offers many scoring options to a team with strong jumpers.

Procedure:

(a) Arrange a team of five at the center circle or the back-court circle, as shown by the diagram.

(b) In Diagram 11a, the jumper taps to a forward, who taps

to a guard breaking fast for a basket or a pass to the other forward. The other guard becomes the safety man.

(c) In Diagram 11b, the jumper taps to one forward, who passes to the other forward. This player can shoot or pass to the breaking guard.

(d) In Diagram 11c, the jumper taps to a forward. This forward passes to the opposite guard, whose man has been screened by the opposite forward.

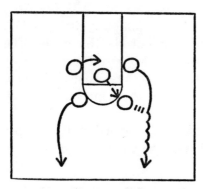

Diagram 11A

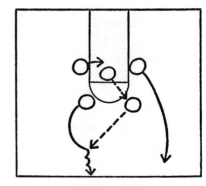

Diagram 11B

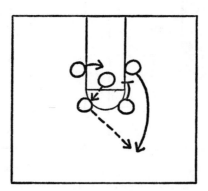

Diagram 11C

17

Out-of-Bounds Drills

The out of bounds situation rightly assumes an important role in most basketball practice sessions. Coaches have seen other teams score two to six baskets a game with well-executed drills from under the basket throw-ins. As a matter of keeping up with the neighbors, every team has several drills of this nature in its repertoire. The out of bounds drill from the sideline has not proved as successful. It is more difficult to execute the screen play to completion before a defense can recover at such a distance from the goal. Most teams have abandoned the side line play completely. Others feel that they should have at least one side line drill for possible emergencies in the closing minutes of a close game. Certainly, such a drill would have merit as a weapon against a press.

Drills are offered here to cover both situations. The coach may use his own judgment about the merits of each and their values to his team. All of these drills will work when run on either side.

1. Drills from the Square Formation

The roll-out, multiple screen and outside screen are all worked well from this formation.

Option 1a:

(a) Arrange a group of five men under one basket as shown in Diagram 1a.

(b) #1 moves across the lane and screens for #2. #2 will break around the screen for a possible pass from #5. #1 pivots rearward and is ready to take the pass right under the basket.

(c) #3 screens for #4, rolls out and becomes a safety. #4 breaks around the screen for a possible pass from #5. The drill can be run when #5 takes the ball from the other side of the floor by having #1, #2, #3 and #4 exchange assignments.

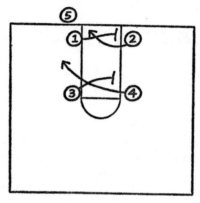

Diagram 1A

Option 1b:

(a) #1, #2 and #3 move to screen for #4. #4 breaks around the screen for a pass from #5.

(b) #2 pivots rearward for the roll-out and a possible pass.

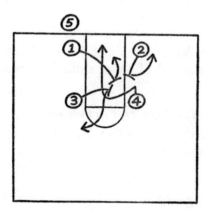

Diagram 1B

#1 pivots to a point directly in front of the goal. #3 moves out to become the safety.

Option 1c:

(a) #1 moves to screen for #3, who breaks around. #2 screens for #4, who breaks around.

(b) #1 becomes the safety and #2 rear pivots to the front of the basket.

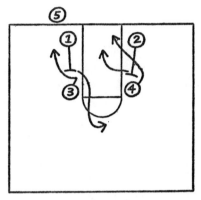

Diagram 1C

2. Drills from the Diamond Formation

The diamond formation offers a number of good drills. Three of the simplest and best are shown here.

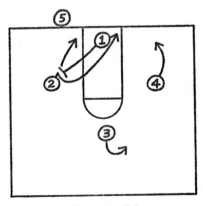

Diagram 2A

Option 2a:

(a) Arrange five men as shown in Diagram 2a.

(b) #1 moves out to set a screen for #2, #3 or #4. In this case he is screening for #2.

(c) The man who is receiving the assistance by way of a screen will break close off the screener for the goal. The screener will roll out and turn toward the goal.

(d) The two men not involved will step back to keep their men occupied.

Option 2b:

(a) #1 moves out to screen for #2. #2 breaks around for a possible pass. #3 breaks inside and screens for #4. #4 breaks around and has the advantage of a set screen from #3 and a moving screen from #2.

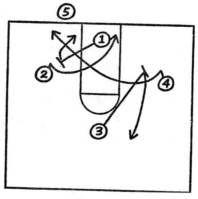

Diagram 2B

(b) After #4 clears, #1 rolls to the goal and #3 drops back as the safety.

Option 2c:

(a) #1 moves out to set a screen for #3. While #1 is setting the screen, #2 and #4 cross fast with #2 going first. As soon as they have crossed, #3 breaks off his screen for the bucket and should be the best bet for a scoring threat.

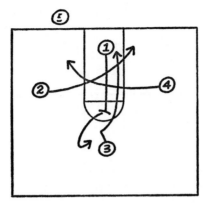

Diagram 2C

3. Drills from the V-Formation

This formation gives the advantage of spreading the defense. This drill has many options, of which three are explained here.

Option 3a:

(a) #1 and #2 cross with #2 going first. #3 and #4 across with #4 going first. #3 should be the open man.

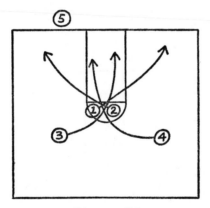

Diagram 3A

Option 3b:

(a) #1 and #2 move to a position side by side on the free throw line.

(b) #3 breaks forward and takes the pass from #5. #4 fakes

in and breaks out to a point directly behind the double set screen set by #1 and #2.

(c) #3 passes to #4 for the shot.

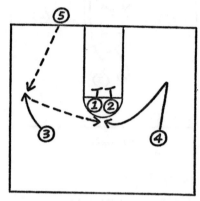

Diagram 3B

Option 3c:

(a) #1, #2, and #3 all break across to set a triple screen for #4. #4 breaks around all of these moving screens for the pass from #5.

(b) #2 goes to the front of the goal. #3 goes to the right side and #1 becomes the safety.

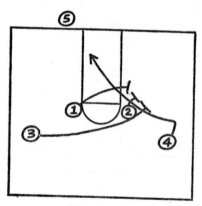

Diagram 3C

4. *Drills from the Parallel Formation*

One of the oldest formations, the parallel line-up still works. It is hard to defend and fun to run.

Option 4a:

(a) Arrange one team of five as the diagram shows.

(b) Any one of the four may drop back to take a shot over the set screen offered by the other three. In this case it is #2.

(c) #1, #3 and 4 close in as #2 drops back and receives the high pass from #5. #2 takes a shot from this position.

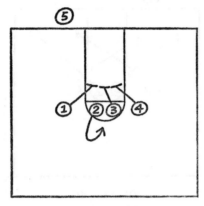

Diagram 4A

Option 4b:

(a) #1, #2 and #3 move to their right and set a moving screen for #4. #4 breaks around and should be open for the pass from #5.

(b) #1 goes in on the right side. #2 goes to the front of the goal and #3 becomes the safety.

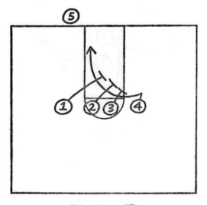

Diagram 4B

Option 4c:

(a) #1 and #2 cross with #2 going first. #3 and #4 cross with #3 going first.

(b) The logical man to hit with the pass should be #1, since he has the advantage of a double screen set by #2 and #4.

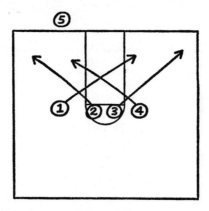

Diagram 4C

5. Drills from the Vertical Formation

This formation is used primarily on the assumption that the defense cannot stay with the offense for the short break.

Option 5a:

(a) #4 breaks in and #1 breaks to the corner as soon as #4 clears his left side.

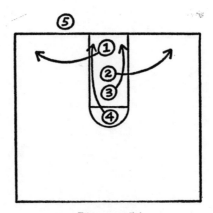

Diagram 5A

(b) #3 breaks to the right side and #2 breaks to the corner as soon as #3 clears his right side.

(c) Either corner man should provide a good receiver. #1 is the receiver here.

Option 5b:

(a) #1 breaks right. #2 breaks left. #3 breaks right and #4 breaks straight for the goal.

(b) #4 should be the open man.

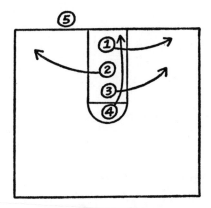

Diagram 5B

Option 5c:

(a) Place the tallest man in the line-up as the #1 man.

(b) #2 and #4 breaks right while #3 breaks left.

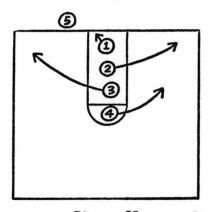

Diagram 5C

(c) #5 gives a lob pass to #1 as close to the front of the rim as possible for an attempt at the tip-in.

6. Drills from the Side Line

These drills are offered mainly as emergency plays. It is possible that one of them might get the bucket that would determine the winner in the late minutes of a close game.

Option 6a:

(a) Arrange five men in position as shown in Diagram 6a.

(b) #3 and #4 cross with #4 going first, #3 takes the pass from #5. #2 breaks out to give #5 a moving screen. After cutting in front of #3, #4 continues on into the left side and gives #1 a moving screen.

(c) #1 moves out to take the pass from #3. #2 rolls out of his screen for #5 and breaks into the left side. #5 breaks in on the right side. #5 should be the open man. #3 remains out as a safety while #4 takes his man to the corner to get him out of the action area.

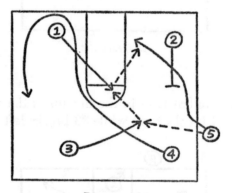

Diagram 6A

Option 6b:

This drill will work best against a team that is pressing all over the court.

(a) #1 and #2 break out to screen for #3 and #4. #2 arrives first and #4 breaks down the side line to take the pass from #5. #1 sets his screen for #3, who breaks down the middle for a pass from #4. #4 is dribbling from the corner.

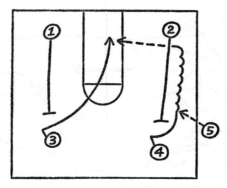

Diagram 6B

7. *Out of Bounds Drill for Pressure Defense*

When a team is pressed, one of its worst enemies (other than the pressure defense) is loss of poise. Confidence and poise can be strengthened by having some system to rely on when the press is applied.

(a) Arrange five players as shown in the diagram.

(b) #1, a forward, takes the ball out of bounds.

(c) At #1's signal #2, the pivot, breaks to screen for #3, a guard. #3 breaks at the same time, receives a moving pick and takes the pass from #1.

(d) #2 moves on down court and hooks back to the head of the circle. #1 breaks left and screens for #5, who has already received a screen from #4. #5 cuts on around and receives a pass from #3, who has taken a dribble or two in his direction.

(e) #5 dribbles down the right side of the floor to a point near center line. Here he passes to #2.

(f) #1, who has received a screen from #4, breaks in on the left side of the floor. Meanwhile #5 cuts in on the right side. #2 may pass to either of them.

(g) If neither cutter is open, they will cross under and take up forward positions. #5 will pass out to #4 or #3, who take the guard positions. #5 drops back to take his regular pivot position and the entire team is ready to function under more nearly normal circumstances.

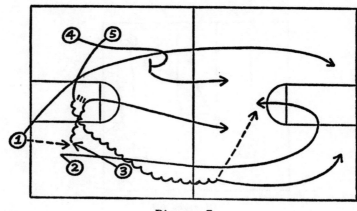

Diagram 7

18

Ball Possession Drills

Although everyone appreciates the fast action associated with basketball, there is a time when it is to the smart team's advantage to slow the game to a walk. There is a time when it is wise to keep ball possession until the game is over. Some of these drills are designed to keep the ball as long as possible. Others are suited for slowing down the game.

1. Chase the Dribbler Drill

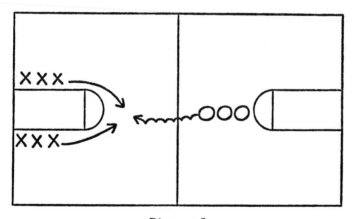

Diagram 1

This is a drill for teaching the dribbler to protect the ball when he is crowded. The team that has a good dribbler can make him better through use of this drill. That same dribbler may be the boy who freezes the ball until the clock runs out for a victory.

219

Procedure:

(a) Place two lines of men under the goal and one line at center court.

(b) The first man from the center court line starts dribbling as he crosses the center line and is met by the first two men from the other line.

(c) The coach, using a stop watch, times the length of time the dribbler keeps possession.

(d) All lines rotate in a counter-clockwise direction and the dribbler keeping possession longest is declared the winner.

2. *Keep-Away Drill*

Pressure is one of the greatest enemies of the team trying to stall the game. To give the team experience at feeling and reacting to this pressure, use this timed keep-away drill.

Procedure:

(a) Divide the squad into groups of five.

(b) Place two groups on the floor and give the ball to one.

(c) The coach times the number of seconds or minutes this group can keep the ball. When they lose possession, allow the defensive team to take a turn at keeping possession.

(d) Keep rotating the groups until every team has had a chance. That team keeping the ball for the longest period of time is the winner.

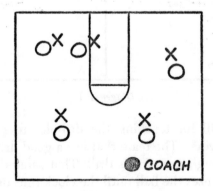

Diagram 2

3. Three Man Freeze Drill

This drill would work well for a team that has three good ball handlers and two fairly large men who are not too adept at dribbling.

Procedure:

(a) Players are arranged as the diagram shows.

(b) #4 starts the drill by moving inside #3 and giving him a handoff. #3 moves to the inside of #5 and gives him a handoff. The three men continue to work a figure eight pattern out front.

(c) Any time one of the three men get in trouble, the tallest deep man, either #1 or #2, breaks to the free throw line to take a pass. This man can fake a pass back to the other deep man and pass back out to one of the outside men, who will continue the freeze.

(d) This drill may be initiated in either direction. Each hand-off man must be careful to avoid contact with the defensive player.

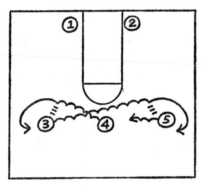

Diagram 3

4. Four Man Weave

This drill will work for the team which has a large pivot man who is a good receiver but not too good at dribbling or cutting.

Procedure:

(a) The players start from the positions shown in the diagram.

(b) #1 passes to #2 and breaks off the left hip of the post. #2 passes to #3 coming out and breaks off the right hip of the post man.

(c) #3 passes to #4 and breaks. #4 passes to #2 who has made a turn to come back out on the left side. The drill moves continuously in this fashion unless the defense is able to halt it. If so, a pass is made into #5, who passes back out, and the drill continues.

(d) The drill may be started to the left or right.

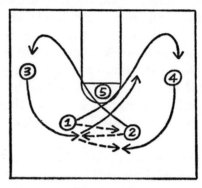

Diagram 4

5. *Five Man Continuity Freeze*

To run this drill successfully, all five men must be good ball handlers, passers and dribblers. If the team has such talent, it is probably the best drill offered here for freezing the ball.

Procedure:

(a) Station five men as the diagram shows.
(b) #2 starts the drill by passing to #1. #2 breaks down the

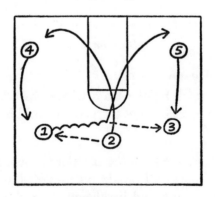

Diagram 5

middle and takes #4's place, who moves out to take #1's place. #1 dribbles to #2's spot and passes to #3. #1 breaks down the middle and takes #5's spot, who moves out to 3#'s vacated position. #3 dribbles to the middle and passes to #4. All players continue to revolve in this fashion.

(c) Any time the drill is jammed, the best dribbler should come to the assistance of the man in trouble. He takes the ball and sets the drill up to start again.

Index

B

M